ABOUT THE BOOK

Duncan Stevens has spent his life working in the field of influence and persuasion. He is a master influencer, founder and director of the Influence Association and travels the world helping brands, companies and individuals to unlock their full potential of effective influence.

Inside the pages of this book, you will find some never-before-shared insights and methods of influence and persuasion that you can apply right now to both your personal and professional life to make you a more influential and effective individual.

If you are looking to order more copies of this book for your team and want to secure bulk prices or inquire about bringing Duncan to your event as a keynote speaker, trainer or, facilitator, then contact Duncan at duncan@duncanstevens.com.

DUNCAN STEVENS

EFFECTIVE INFLUENCE

65 INFLUENCE BASED EXPERIMENTS EXPLAINED

TO MAKE YOU MORE EFFECTIVE

THE INFLUENCE ASSOCIATION

Copyright © 2021 by Duncan Stevens

All rights reserved. No part of this book may be reproduced, stored in a retrieval system, or transmitted in any form or by any means, without the prior or written consent of the publisher, except in the case of brief quotations embodied in reviews and articles. Any person who does any unauthorized act in relation to this publication may be liable to criminal prosecution and civil claims for damages.

Influence Association

www.influenceassociation.com

Duncan Stevens

www.duncanstevens.com

A CIP catalogue record for this book is available from the British Library.

ISBN: 978-1-8383799-4-0

Produced by the Influence Association

Editing by the Influence Association

Cover and interior design by the Influence Association

CONTENTS

SHARE THE POWER OF EFFECTIVE INFLUENCE

My wish is that you'll read this book to the end and implement some or all of the ideas in your own life. Even if you only action a few tips, I'm 100% confident that you will become far more effective in your personal, social and professional life.

At the end of the book, feel free to pass it on to someone else to help them become a more effective manager, parent, sales-person or business owner too. Alternatively, donate it to a charity shop, leave it in a coffee shop or even on a train for someone else to pick up. Maybe scrawl your name and email address on the inside cover to connect with like-minded people.

If you want to have the comfort of knowing that you can refer back to it, just lend it out. Even if it ends up in the hands of someone else, if you pop on over to our website and drop us a message about what you thought of the book, we'll send you some free updates when they come out too!

Duncan Stevens

www.duncanstevens.com

THE IMPORTANCE OF INFLUENCE

Every day we are either influencing or being influenced. Whether we realise it or not, this is one of the many transactions we are having with life. In business, we use influence to accomplish two things; either we want to influence others to buy our products or services or, we want to influence ourselves or our teams to improve our or their effectiveness. Essentially, our effectiveness is directly proportional to our ability to influence the people around us.

In today's age, influence is a metaphorical currency that we can use to grow ourselves or our businesses.

Even the term influencer has virtually been monetized. If you have a certain number and type of followers and create appropriate content, companies will pay influencers big money to promote their brands, products, or services. Online influence has never been so monetized. Being an influencer online is simply an extension to influencing people, companies, businesses, or prospective clients offline.

In the current digital age dominated by social media, companies and brands often turn to specialists to influence others to purchase their products or services. If these influence techniques are executed correctly, this will lead to more clients, more profit and increased brand awareness and visibility in your market.

Individually, the most successful way to create influence is by being influential. Let's take a 'hypothetical example' of the American elections. Let's say you could influence your electorate into voting for you to become the next President. The influence you would then hold as a result of winning would be even greater.

If we were to apply that same idea to our own lives, if I was to introduce you to my friends as being an incredible human being, with a great circle of friends, warm, hospitable and generous, with a great sense of humour, I would be influential in painting a picture to everyone else about your personality. In doing so, I would increase my own influence even further. A compliment like this, if delivered with authenticity and honesty, activates the reciprocity principle of persuasion that we will cover later – in that people will feel indebted to pay that gift of a compliment back to us at a later date. Their reciprocation of this may not come in the form of another compliment but something larger and more beneficial to our own success.

Whether you are persuading people to vote for you in the next election or merely giving someone a compliment, influence is essentially encouraging people to think or act as you do. In today's society of social media, there has never been a greater opportunity to reach more people than ever before. With the emphasis on the 'social' element of social media, people can equally build groups, communities, followers and 'tribes' who can spread their messages to others.

This means that our persuasive messages can reach further than ever before. It also means that we have the potential to influence more people than ever before too. On an individual level, as we begin to see more and more people having some form of influence on society, it is apparent that influence does not come from titles or hierarchies within an organization.

Instead, influence is now created by your credibility, by refining your message and then passionately sharing it in innovative and creative ways. This has since been associated with the relatively new word of 'virality' where an idea, concept, or message spreads like wildfire and reaches a maximum audience. If people who have been exposed to this content, idea or message, and enjoy it, then they may very well become 'follower' or 'fans'. This reiterates the idea that you can simply create influence by being influential.

Much like the law of inertia, influence is an action that starts and then maintains motion until something pushes or pulls on it. Therefore, people with strong persuasive abilities can influence those people who are open to being influenced (starting the motion) and then propel them forward once they are engaged (maintaining the motion).

Influence also allows you to build a community. To ensure that your community supports you in the most difficult of times, it's important to create a level of commitment beyond the surface level. By nurturing existing connections and building new relationships, allows you to grow your community and ensure they are both loyal and strong brand ambassadors for you too. By doing this, your loyal community will reciprocate the leadership you have shown them and support you through difficult times to ensure a higher chance that your brand or company will be able to weather any metaphorical storms which would otherwise destroy others with a less loyal fan or community base.

With a loyal community, you can celebrate your victories but equally support each other in the losses. When you ask most people what they want out of life, one of the most common replies is 'I want to be happy'. Happiness is one of the few things in life which increases when it is shared. Thus it is far more satisfying to reach your goal or outcome with a group than by yourself. Having the ability to persuade and influence people effectively (either online or offline) will ensure that both you and your community will be more effective and achieve a greater level of success too.

WHAT INFLUENCE IS NOT

Being an influencer is a term that is given to people on Instagram who create and curate their own content and build a large following – to influence others. Their followers' have been influenced to follow them by being attracted to their lifestyle choices, habits, clothes, fashion and other elements. Despite this – the word 'influencer' is not solely restricted to Instagram. Being influential, having the ability to influence or being an influencer are verbs, all born from the same verb - 'to influence'. You can exert influence on your friends, family, partner, social situation, work, or you can even self-influence.

By learning and applying the principles, models, methods and techniques detailed in this book, I guarantee you will be significantly more effective in your life. All the principles and practices explained within and supported by peer reviews, studies, research and experiments can help you create the life you desire, help you attain your dreams and goals, and essentially bring increased joy into your life.

Throughout this book, you will read experiments and research to help us understand why we act the way that we do, why we react differently in different situations to others, and why we buy or follow specific trends, fashions, and more.

One can undoubtedly reap much higher rewards by developing and improving one's influence and persuasion skills. For others who are simply bystanders to this self-development, influencing to gain personal and financial benefits can sometimes be perceived as a covert form of manipulation. It's not. Unfortunately, the word 'manipulation' has taken on negative connotations, with manipulation being regarded as a more sinister form of influence. If you were to take the example of a surgeon's knife – it can both save a life and be used as a weapon to destroy a life. A surgeon's knife, much like the word 'influence', 'persuasion' or 'manipulation', is simply a neutral term. It's what you do with that neutral term that determines the connotations you give it.

When people use a specific skill set for bad, then that word takes on a negative meaning. Another example is the 'Occult'. Historically, spiritual gurus used the methodologies used in the Occult for good but slowly, it became used for evil over time and then glamorized in movies.

So whilst the word 'manipulation' may have negative connotations, if you are trying to manipulate someone who has lung cancer to stop smoking as an example, surely this is more associated with positivity and good. We generally lend the word 'manipulation' to the notion when someone is using their influence to achieve selfish means. Influence does not do use psychological manipulation or tricks, nor does it involve using bribes, subterfuge, or deceit to get your desired result or goal.

In fact, the most effective mindset to approach influence or persuasion is to place other people's wants, needs, and desires on an equal footing to your own.

WHAT INFLUENCE IS

As the title suggests, this book focuses on effective influence.

Influence, in its distilled form, is essentially 'conveying a set of values by example that affects the opinions, actions and behaviours of others'.

For example, if you are a sports personality, if you adhere to the rules of etiquette on and off the pitch (or track) both in your private and public life, you can influence those around you to aspire to be like you. If you don't meet or convey these sets of values and your reputation becomes tarnished, you will soon see that your level of influence dwindles. Take Tiger Woods as an example. He is widely regarded as one of the greatest athletes of all time. As a result, he commands a broad portfolio of sponsorship deals. Many brands and companies aspire to be associated with the Tiger Woods brand. Tiger's brand had been initially built around himself as a superb athlete from a young age, with a graceful approach to the sport and respectable private life. The fact that so many brands wanted to align with him speaks volumes of the level of influence he held over his fans, with the sponsors knowing that they would have an extremely high return on investment.

However when, in 2010, after a series of alleged extramarital affairs and a drink driving car accident, several of Tiger's sponsors severed ties with him and his brand. Over the course of that scandal-plagued year, AT&T, Accenture, Gatorade and Gillette all dropped their sponsorship deals with him due to his tarnished image.

Not only do a sport's stars values influence their supporters and fans, but detrimental behaviours such as the ones mentioned above can influence people's opinions of the brands or sponsors that they align themselves with. In Tigers case, AT&T, Accenture, Gatorade and Gillette all wanted to preserve their own image that they had crafted for their followers and fans and left when this was tarnished.

WHAT PERSUASION IS

The words persuasion and influence are often used interchangeably, but there is a difference. Having outlined what influence is earlier, persuasion is the process of 'achieving aligned objectives'. Persuasion differs from influencing in that you are spurring somebody to make certain decisions without actually earning their genuine buy-in. Influence, on the other hand, is a much more finessed process, with the need to win their heart or mind in order to inspire them to take action or make a particular decision.

Persuasion in the sales arena focuses on a win-win outcome to a transaction. For example, if I decide to sell my house and you want to buy my house, an effective persuader will ensure that both parties close the transaction happy with the outcome. Persuasion always involves personal interaction, unlike influence, where this is not always necessary. Brands can influence you to buy something without having ever directly interacted with you. Persuasion uses both spoken and written words, reasoned arguments, anecdotes and stories, emotive appeals, subliminal cues, fact-based evidence, the evocation of specific memories, the use of colour and imagery, expert opinion, gestures, expressions, logic, repetition, and more.

Whilst you can use persuasive or influence strategies in a manipulative or self-serving manner to reach an agreement, you will find that you will only be able to use this tactic once.

After this, the prospective client or customer will realise that your influence strategy has only been self-serving, and you will see a fast deterioration of the relationship. Manipulative techniques can similarly come back to bite you if there has been some trickery or foul play involved.

So whether you call it influence, persuasion or manipulation, the difference is simply down to your intent. If you place your prospect's wants and needs on an equal footing to your own and uphold your own ethical values with a focus on a win-win relationship as opposed to win-lose, you will not only be able to negotiate much more effectively but be able to nurture that relationship and give yourself room for future interaction and negotiation.

The good news is the art of influence and persuasion can be taught and learnt. The bad news is, there is no silver bullet or three magic words to instantly give you influence. But with a little application, and if you make it to the end of this book, you will certainly have the tools, techniques and mindset to influence both yourself and others around you. With practice, you will find yourself becoming more and more influential and realise that the distance between success and failure gets shorter and shorter as you become more and more effective.

SO, WHO AM I?

My name is Duncan Stevens, and for the past ten years, I've been travelling Europe, Asia, and America, sharing my intimate knowledge about influence and persuasion with some of the world's most respected companies and brands. I present keynote speeches and offer influence and leadership training at conferences, marketing and sales events and other corporate functions. In addition, I help small and large teams to work more effectively using influence and persuasion techniques. I show clients how they can supercharge their influence skills both online and offline in a world where it's becoming increasingly important to stand out and make true connections.

However, I've not always been a globe-trotting influence consultant and speaker. My early years were spent working on the most challenging of coal faces; Sales – cold calling people to persuade and influence them to make donations to the particular charity I was representing. I also plied my trade cold calling door-to-door to encourage donations. In both, I excelled. Not only did I excel, but in the time that I was influencing cold-leads to sign up to the charity to donate regularly, I secured the most charitable donations from cold and warm leads across the whole company (spread across multiple sites in the UK). All employees were given the same training and the same tools to use, but some failed to last the probationary period whilst others like me shone. Although this may sound like I am blowing my own horn, and to some extent I am, but it was then that

I realised that this was something I loved and was great at. I felt if I could be great at something like persuasion, with no prior experience, then I could teach it.

Despite this, even at that earlier stage in my career, I realised that whilst influencing people to sign up for donations was worthwhile, it wasn't my calling. That said, it did spark something inside of me, and I soon moved into a sales and coaching arena and, at the same time, was performing after-dinner influence-based mentalism shows. Even now, I still get hired by clients to perform my mentalism stage show at corporate events and conferences. My show does rely heavily on some of the influence skillsets I'm going to divulge to you in this book, but these skills are equally applicable and transferable into the world of sales, marketing, business, leadership, and motivation.

Several years ago, someone approached me at the end of a show. They invited me to come to their business and share some of my influence and persuasion techniques and methods with their colleagues by delivering a keynote address and training day. Fast forward several more years, and that first event keynote and workshop have since become a much more polished offering that I am incredibly proud of. Armed with my background in teaching and coaching (in a different field), I began to work on my offering as it is now.

Fast forward ten years, and I have distilled down the core principles of influence and breathed new life and perspective into them. When I present at a masterclass, training day, sales kick-off, or conference, you can be confident that all the techniques and methodologies I share are all underpinned by real-life evidence-based research and experiments, some of which you will find in this book.

It means that you and your teams can apply them straight away and experience a real shift in effectiveness either at home or at work.

When I'm not conducting corporate talks, training sessions, or influence shows, I offer more personal assistance to those who seek out my services. I occasionally have the pleasure of coaching people to help find and realise their purpose or mission in life using some of the techniques shared in this book. Whilst these more private consultations may not sound as glamourous as speaking in the Middle East or running a masterclass in America, they certainly give me the most satisfaction.

Whilst I simply couldn't fit over ten years of knowledge about influence and persuasion into this one book, the techniques and skills I outline here will not only make you more effective in your personal and work life but will also complement and supercharge your existing knowledge about influence. It is also my hope that it will encourage you to look at the art of influence in a new light and see it as less of a technique and more of an art form.

SO, WHY THIS BOOK?

Influence is one of those intriguing subjects which people often say – "I can't be influenced" or "That wouldn't happen to me" or "I just buy those products and services because I want to, or "I just like them".

Influence has now become synonymous with decision-making and extends far beyond a company encouraging you to buy a certain dress from a certain company as an example. The power of influence has been wielded to place a new President in the White House or Prime Minister on the steps of Downing Street. Influence is the factor that has determined whether the UK voted to stay in the European Union or leave it. The same persuasive techniques are at play online too. Influence encourages us to follow certain people on social media who lack any discernible talent, skills or authority. We follow them, like their posts, buy their products, share their views, and even shape our own lives to be similar to theirs. The persuasive power of these social media icons is such that they are known to the world as 'influencers'.

Whether you are using influence to sway the opinion of an electorate or bring followers to your social media account or any other situation where you want to change behaviour or actions in others, a similar selection of techniques and processes are used. Behind all of this, we still believe our choices are our own. The principle of 'influence without awareness' is integral to the success of the experiments shared in this book. Of course, we can look back in hindsight and justify our reasons for acting or thinking a certain way, but we are simply part of an ongoing transaction of influence with the world. We are both influencing and being influenced. Both are happening consciously and subconsciously.

Whenever I read books or watch documentaries that describe behavioural or social psychology tests that focus on influence as their core theme, I am often left thinking – would I have acted the same way? Am I easily influenced? Of course, many of these experiments and tests are situational, relying heavily on the interaction or interjection of others. The situations are often controlled, and our responses may be very different in that situation. Take the stress response; 'fight or flight' where if we are faced with danger, some of us will stay and try and resolve that situation (fight) whilst others will turn our backs and leave it to someone else to deal with. (Flight)

Many of us would want to see ourselves as the kind of people who would stay and help others out of a potentially dangerous situation. The reality is that when we are safe behind the pages of a book or behind a television screen, our confidence levels are high, and our reactions will be much more distorted than if we are actually in that particular situation.

That said, all the experiments in this book pose a question first. When I pose similar questions in my talks, delegate responses are very much in keeping with some of the participants involved in the experiments. As a result, this gives you a great acid test as to how you would be influenced in a given situation and allows you to reflect on why you made that choice instead of the other.

Often when we read experiments or tests in behavioural psychology books, we find ourselves questioning our own response. 'I wouldn't do that' or 'I wouldn't behave like that' or 'I'd make a different choice' are certain thoughts I would have. I found that others did too. Because of that, I wanted to give the reader the opportunity to make those choices for themselves before revealing what the conclusion the researchers came to at the end of the experiment. This will, give you the opportunity to almost participate remotely in all 65 experiments.

Some of the techniques and ideas that form the basis for these experiments can be broken down into principles and then applied in your work or personal life. In previous books I have read, I have found experiments, anecdotes, and information muddled or incoherent and littered with extensive and tedious research papers, where all I wanted to do was find what was learned and how can I apply this to make me more effective.

After years of collation, research and evaluation of various influence and persuasion based experiments, I wanted to present some of the core principles and approaches to influence in a clear and coherent way. In doing so, I hope that when you have read them, you can think about how these experiments and principles are applicable to your work, social, or personal life and how they can be applied and employed to deliver maximum effectiveness.

If we are operating more effectively, then we will feel happier both within ourselves and with those around us. In the past, I have only been able to share my knowledge and research, and principles with a certain number of people in a year, so this book gives me the perfect opportunity to share my passion with a much wider and broader audience. Now I obviously can't include all of the principles and research from over ten years into this one book but what I can do is give you an abridged version that is easily digestible and applicable directly to your own lives. With that set, let's dive straight in.

AN OVERVIEW

Influence and persuasion are fundamentally driven by the behavioural science principles of psychology. As you will see in this book, regardless of whether we have the same income level, job, family, lifestyle, interests, or hobbies, we all have a different perspective on the world. A different perspective means that we are all influenced in a different way.

Imagine for a second you had used your newfound influencing skills to secure a fantastic new house overlooking the sea with your own private beach. In your frustration at seeing holiday makers wander across your' newly purchased beach front plot, you decide to erect a sign.

Take the example of the wording on the two signs below.

PRIVATE BEACH - PRIVATE PROPERTY BEYOND THIS POINT

And

WARNING SHARK SIGHTED – KEEP OUT

Some may be more influenced by one than the other. Conversely, some people may have a complete disregard for both signs. The first sign is a more informational form of communication in that it seeks to inform people's attitudes. The second is a more behavioural form of communication that has a deeper motivation and more compelling argument.

The very idea that you would use the same message or communication style to all women, or all Asians, or all people who read the Financial Times is absurd.

The idea of using a 'one size fits' all approach to influence would render your approach highly ineffective. Whilst you could certainly segment and target your influence message based on geography, demographics, consumer and lifestyle attributions, media consumption, diet, music, or TV viewing tastes, your impact would be far more powerful if you also considered personality traits. It is our personality that informs our decision-making and drives the products we buy or services we choose.

In fact, Aristotle, the Greek Philosopher, and student of Plato said:

"Character may almost be called the most effective means of persuasion."

THE 5-POINT PERSONALITY MODEL

As I mentioned previously, I am regularly hired as a keynote speaker to give talks and demonstrations using my intimate knowledge of people as to how we can influence others. If you have been to one of my performances or speeches, you may have seen one of my demonstrations of influence. One of the most astonishing for members of the audience is when I invite a participant on stage to don a blindfold and then hold a big rock in their hands. Using a technique I have honed and developed called 'Influence without awareness', I can get them to genuinely describe that they are feeling the softness and roughness of a sponge. When they look down (and to the rest of the audience), they see that they are, in fact, holding a big heavy rock. This experiment can be repeated many times, but I keep it to just two or three demonstrations. With the second, the person is describing that they feel a small silver teaspoon in their hands, and when they lift the blindfold off their eyes, they will see that, in fact, it is a large soup ladle.

One of the core applications of influence that I use in this routine and one which also informs decision making when it comes to buying a product or service or even voting is 'personality analysis'. Having been a psychological illusionist and master of influence for the best part of 10 years, I have honed the ability to be able to identify peoples key personality traits in a very short space of time.

We all exhibit a wide range of personality traits. In fact, psychologist Gordon Allport, and one of the founding figures of personality psychology, identified that we exhibit 4,000 of them.

Preceding this comprehensive study, Raymond Cattell had identified 16 dimensions of human personality, whilst Hans Eysenck's created a three-factor personality theory. Eysenck identified these traits as psychoticism, extraversion, and neuroticism and their bipolar opposites.

Many researchers agree that Cattell's theory was far too complicated, Eysenk's was too limited in its scope, and Allport's theory was too detailed. As a result, the 5-factor theory emerged off the back of these to describe the range of traits that form the building blocks of our personality. This was later coined 'The Big Five' with O.C.E.A.N as its acronym.

It is these five core personality types that I look out for in my initial interaction with a participant. By combining this quick evaluation of their personality with other more subtle influence techniques (some of which I share with you in the book), I am able to influence participants' actions and behaviours, such as influencing them to describe the feeling of a sponge when they are just holding a rock. (I must also add that there is no hypnosis or embedded suggestion in my work, just the intimate and covert use of influence which we will talk about later on).

Making an assessment of the 5-factor personality traits[1] of the person you want to influence when it comes to the subtle art of influence and persuasion is absolutely key.

Thus, with no further delay, here is the 5-factor personality model:

Openness – Are they open-minded and authority challenging?

Conscientiousness – Are they self-disciplined and prefer structure, plans and order?

Extraversion – Do they enjoy spending time with others?

Agreeableness – Are they warm, friendly and place other people's needs before their own?

Neurotic – Do they tend to worry a lot?

As I mentioned earlier, if you send the same message to different people in the same demographic, they may have very different world views. To give you an example as to how this would translate to different personality types:

An open person may be more sociable and therefore more likely influenced by the views of others in their own peer group or social circle

A conscientious person may be more ordered and therefore more influenced by a rational, fact-based argument.

An extroverted person often seeks to engage with experiences and to respond to excitement or attention.

An agreeable person may be more altruistic and tend to put the community and society needs ahead of their own, being influenced by those in their community or society.

A neurotic person may be more heavily influenced by an emotional message.

SEGMENTATION

All 5 of these people may all be from the same neighbourhood, all Caucasian, of a similar level of affluence, and at first glance may look similar on the surface, but in fact, often want and respond to two completely different things. Let's imagine I have created a brand new vegan chocolate bar. Let's also assume I have decided that my target audience is female, aged between 20-37 years old, married with children, and reads The Daily Mail.

Traditional ways to influence this group would be for one generic message for all women who fall into this category. In the 1950s, examples of this may include 'Beanz Meanz Heinz.' This is more of a creative-led form of communication from the top-down, simply hoping that your creative ideas create the desired influence.

Much more recently, ways to influence people have become much more audience-led, as agencies and creative teams have access to unparalleled levels of consumer data harvested from our online footprints. Using this data, it's possible to exert an even greater level of influence over our target audience by offering a much more granular and bespoke approach to influence.

Our female target audience for our vegan chocolate bar may look very similar on the outside, but their worldview could be completely different. As a result, their influence triggers will vary too. For example, both may want to buy our vegan chocolate bar, but one may be health-conscious and not want any refined, processed sugar in their diet, whilst the other is more environmentally focussed and would want it without dairy or palm oil. With this knowledge in mind, the creative, communication, advert, or influencing medium could be tailored accordingly.

But it's not just personality that we can use to influence people. Demographic and geographic information can also assist us in making a targeted approach to influence.

In doing so, we can consider:

- Age
- Gender
- Ethnicity
- Religion
- Education
- Income
- Home owner
- Socio Economic status
- Geographic factors

These are more fact-based attributes. So whilst they aren't as varied as 'personality types,' they do provide crucial information to help pinpoint our target market. Attitudes, on the other hand, do require much more finessing. Personality traits are heavily influenced by the following attitudinal traits:

- Advertising resonance – What kind of magazines you read?
- Automotive data - what car you drive?
- Consumer data

- Consumer confidence - Economy / Business
- Lifestyle Data – What loyalty club you belong to?
- What are their buying styles/patterns?
- Civic / political engagement segments - What church you attend?
- Cellular / mobile packages types and level of usage?

Knowing this information alongside the other pieces of information can influence the way that you vote or the products and services you buy.

Taking into account peoples' activities, interests, and opinions (commonly called AIO's for short by marketing executives) and their previously mentioned behaviours and attitudes, people can be influenced through 6 persuasion principles. These include:

- Reciprocity
- Scarcity
- Authority
- Consistency
- Liking
- Consensus

It is the application of these six persuasion principles that can influence and persuade others. Many of the outcomes of the subsequent experiments are underpinned by one or more of these principles of persuasion, so this overview will hopefully lay a good foundation for further evaluation.

RECIPROCITY

Reciprocity is the idea that if you give something to someone, then they will feel indebted to return that favour further down the line in one form or another. The sheer persuasive power of reciprocity is such that even if we don't like the person, we can still give them something, and they will still feel indebted to us. More often than not, they will return the favour at a higher expense even when we don't ask for a favour to be returned. Not only will any favour that is given be highly likely to be reciprocated, but research shows that the very act of us giving a gift to someone else makes us like them even more.

If you wanted to make this extremely powerful persuasion principle even more effective, then it's worth considering making the gift both personalised and unexpected. I know of a fantastic entertainer who had been booked for a private corporate event through an agency for a client. He had never worked for this agency before and was keen to work more. You can imagine to his dismay when he found out that the agency booker was not at the event to allow him to introduce himself in person and showcase his performance to her. It was revealed that a few days before, one of her family members had passed away, and she had taken some time off work to grieve. Instead of leaving the interaction there and or calling up later to pass on his condolences, he did something both personalized and unexpected. He bought a candle and condolences card and posted them out to her with a handwritten note. This was done with authenticity, care and consideration. Two days later, he received an email. The booker was overwhelmed by the thoughtful and generous gift, admitting that not only was it her favourite candle brand but her favourite scent too. He later went on to establish himself as that company's go-to entertainer when his type of act was requested.

But a gift doesn't always have to be physical, nor does it have to be paid for. The act of reciprocity is only limited to your imagination. You could share information, help or advice, give away free tickets to an event, send out a birthday card or more. Whatever you give, the receiver will feel that not only do you care, but you value them and your relationship too.

A significant amount of research shows that carrying out a favour for someone first often results in the opposite party giving significantly more in return in the form of reciprocation. Giving a favour also has its strongest effect when the two parties don't know one another that well, and the gift is small but thoughtful and unexpected. However, research has shown that giving a gift that is too big or generous may cause the recipient to feel overwhelmed and uncomfortable in returning the favour. Above all, a gift or favour should be given with a high degree of authenticity. Whether you are giving a candle, a box of chocolates, a thank you card, or even remembering their birthday, this will ensure people around you feel highly valued – which is an important commodity when influencing others.

Throughout this book, you will read many experiments involving examples of reciprocity and the powerful role it can play in the effectiveness of your business, negotiation, and in any form of a situation requiring influence. Whilst many of the experiments detailed in this book are conducted on participants in America, psychologist Michael Morris and his team looked at how the principle of reciprocity applied to countries. Morris and his team used the multinational bank 'Citibank'[2] for this experiment. In Citibank offices around the world, the formal structure of the organization has little variation across national operations. However, the one variable is that the employees are local to the area. As a result, these Citibank locations provide a natural experiment to test how culture shapes employees' informal interactions and feelings of obligation. They surveyed multiple branches around the world and researched the employee's willingness to comply with a request from a co-worker, specifically for assistance with a task.

They found that in the United States, the negotiation took on a market-based approach and offered assistance based on the normal unofficial rules for reciprocal exchange, with the internal question being "has the person helped me in the past?"

In China, the rules of reciprocation took on a more family-based approach. In a society that encourages loyalty to their work groups, the Chinese were more influenced by the status of their co-worker. This led to the internalised dialogue of "Is this requester connected to someone in my unit, especially someone of higher authority?"

In Spain, negotiation took on a more friendship-based approach, with the internal dialogue being "Is the requester connected to my friends?"

Meanwhile, in Germany, negotiation takes on a more systematic-based approach. Germans base their rules of negotiation on existing norms and rules of association. The internal dialogue in Germany is "according to official rules and categories, am I supposed to assist this request?"

Although the rules of reciprocation differ slightly within each country, between each country, it is still evident that the most fundamental rules apply. Even a country can feel a psychological burden if it doesn't repay a favour, and this is a societal belief more than a cultural one. This is evidenced most clearly in 1985 when Ethiopia was overcome by poverty, starvation and disease. They were struggling to care for their own civilians. However, that same year, they donated $5,000 worth of aid to Mexico City to its victims who had just experienced a major earthquake. The reason they made such a generous donation was because 50 years earlier, in 1935, when Italy had invaded Ethiopia, it was Mexico who sent aid to them. The 1985 earthquake, all those years later, was Ethiopia's opportunity to reciprocate the generosity shown by Mexico. Psychologist John Stacey Adams developed his equity theory in the 1960s, and it can be equally applied to international reciprocation, too, in that we are always trying to pay back offers we receive in order to re-establish equality.

President John F. Kennedy once famously said, "Ask not what your country can do for you. Ask what you can do for your country."

SCARCITY

The fear of loss is more powerful than the fear of gain. If you can communicate this when you are attempting to persuade or influence somebody, then this creates urgency for them to purchase your product, service, or buy-in to your idea. This encourages them to act now through the fear of missing out.

The idea of scarcity is pervasive in all parts of our lives, and for me personally, I know eBay plays the scarcity card beautifully well. If you are anything like me and have had an item on your eBay watch list for the last few days, when it comes to the last few moments and a flurry of bids come in, your heart starts racing for the fear that you will miss out. This is accompanied by the excitement that you could win, too. When you place your bid, you mentally trick yourself into thinking the item is yours, and the more bids that come in, the more you desire it and fear you are going to miss out on it.

Pre-eBay era, in 1973, movie mogul Barry Diller, a negotiation expert at ABC, paid $3.3 million for Poseidon Adventure on TV, which at the time was an obscene amount for any rights purchase. The reason for such a high price tag was that this was the first time any rights had been sold to networks in an open bid auction. An open bid allowed competitors to see each other's bids, and this was the catalyst for a bidding war that resulted in Diller paying over the odds for the rights. He was later quoted, saying that ABC would no longer take part in auctions again.

In similarity to Barry Diller, when we are on a hotel room booking site and see that there are only two rooms left, we get caught up in the idea that we are about to miss out, which prompts us to take action. Similarly, we may be looking to book our flights abroad, and again companies use a similar persuasion principle and suggest that there is a limited supply of seats available. We are influenced by the fear of missing out on something which is presented as 'scarce'. When opportunities become scarce, we desire them more.

Just the idea of scarcity is incredibly powerful too. Take the recent Coronavirus pandemic as an example. Here in the UK, people believed that if we were told to self-isolate, the most important things they should stock up on were rice, pasta, hand sanitisers, and toilet paper. In the first few days, when the UK government declared a state of emergency and lockdown, consumers bought all of the aforementioned items in bulk. This created scarcity. For those who had plenty they were then unsure when they would be able to buy these items next and got caught up in the stockpiling rush too. It became a vicious cycle, people paying over the odds for items that had only been made scarce by people panic buying. In turn, this led to others buying the remainder of the stock. All of these actions came despite the assurances of both the government and supermarkets that their supply chains were strong and working well, and if everybody remained consistent in their buying patterns, there would be no shortages. Thus it was just the idea of scarcity that caused people to act on that notion and create scarcity as a side effect.

English writer and philosopher GK Chesterton once said, "The way to love anything is to realize it might be lost" Adjectives such as 'exclusive', 'rare' or 'limited edition' are all synonymous with scarcity and imply a greater worth and value. Scarcity is used prolifically in bricks and mortar stores with notices such as "Closing down sale", Last ones left", "2 weeks left," etc.

If you can influence your prospective client to imagine that they will miss out on something, this will increase their desire to buy so much more, making scarcity as a principal of persuasion a formidable tool.

An even greater powerful persuasive principle that overpowers people's desire is when something is banned or forbidden. For some, it makes them feel that they have had their liberties taken away from them, which is an extremely powerful motivator. Forbidden or banned information, in many ways, is even more desirable than products and services.

It is widely recognised that juries are influenced by censored information. If a jury finds out that an insurance company will pay any bill for damages, they tend to award larger damages to the plaintiffs. Not only that, but they are known to award even greater damages and compensation pay-outs if they are expressly told by the judge to ignore the fact that the defendant has insurance.

AUTHORITY

People are more quickly influenced by others whom they believe to be credible or reliable experts in their field. A doctor, for example, holds a title which he or she has had to study for, often for many years. We trust them to make the correct assessment of our illness or ailment and offer the correct treatment. We do this in blind faith simply because they sit in a doctor's surgery and hold a certificate. We have also been brought up to follow the process – if you feel unwell, go and see the doctor.

Yet, whilst they have studied for many years to learn how to cure us of our ailment, they may not have the training or expertise to cure our underlying health condition. Our ailment may, perhaps, be better treated by the correct nutrition and attention to our diet. For this, a nutritional therapist would be the more appropriate health practitioner. They, too, have had to study for many years, and their approach may be more beneficial than a doctor as they examine the underlying condition with more rigour.

However, simply due to the authority a doctor holds and our perception of them as being the most credible and reliable experts in the field of healthcare, we place our utmost trust in them, trusting that they are the most capable of treating our condition.

You will read some incredible experiments later in the book, and in one, how simply by wearing a white lab coat and assuming a position of authority, you can influence people to commit the most heinous acts on one another.

The actor Robert Young played the titular lead role of 'Doctor' in the American medical drama, Marcus Welby, from 1969 to 1976. He was recruited to be the face of the Sanka Coffee brand – a non-caffeinated coffee. Due to the fact that he was associated with Doctor Marcus Welby in the popular TV show, this gave him the credibility to be the face of Sanka Coffee. It allowed him to speak about the dangers of caffeine and the benefits of the caffeine-free coffee brand, and viewers believed him. As a result, the series of ads were extremely successful. Actors who play the role of medical professionals are often used in adverts for products simply because people associate the authority the character holds in a TV show to the brand they represent.

In day-to-day life, waiters also demonstrate their authority in a restaurant by recommending a particular bottle of wine. Often this is a more expensive choice, yet we are swayed by their recommendation as we perceive them as an authority on wine, simply because they are working in the restaurant. Rarely will a waiter or waitress be an expert on wine unless they are a sommelier.

Of course, it's relatively easy to convey authority by influencing people's perception, but this won't stand up to scrutiny in the long term. You can also share relevant stories about what others think about you, your product, brand, or service to convey authority. However, if these same stories are shared by others, this adds even greater credibility to your position of authority.

The same can be true for conveying to others the authority that your product or service holds in the marketplace. It is to convey this same message, in the third person using examples such as:

"I'm not going to tell you to buy something just because it's the highest quality and market leader....."

or

"I'm not suggesting that you engage in our services purely because we have won the industry-standard awards for the last two years and offer the best value for money in the industry...."

These kinds of statements create strong emotions within us, and it is emotions that support our behaviours, decisions and actions.

Using authority as a principle of persuasion should never be dismissed when considering how to influence. We have been raised to be obedient to authority - whether it is one's parents, the law, the police or even to religious teachings telling us to behave or not behave in a certain way.

We are led to believe that acting or behaving in a certain way in accordance with law, respect, teachings or principles results in a more harmonious society. Indeed it does, and it is this indoctrination that generally still prevails when we are exposed to authority later in our lives. However, if we want to protect ourselves from the persuasive power of an authority figure, it is worth considering whether they are a reliable, credible, authoritative figure or simply masquerading as one.

CONSISTENCY

Stevens James, the American philosopher and psychologist, once said:

"I don't sing because I'm happy. I'm happy because I sing."

Similar to the conditioning effects that authority has had on our lives from a young age, the same can be drawn from the consistency principle of persuasion. We have been raised to follow a particular trajectory in life. Go to school, get good grades, go to university, get a good job, get married, and have children. Consistency is drilled into us at an early age. We go to bed at a certain time, wake at a certain time, and follow a similar daily routine. For those who are inconsistent in their actions and behaviours, they are synonymous with being flaky, undependable or even untrustworthy. This is in contrast with someone who is consistent in their actions and behaviours. They are seen as being reliable, desirable, and someone who follows through on their plans.

This makes consistency one of the most powerful forces in the human personality, for once we commit to something, we have a hardwired need to remain consistent with that decision, choice, or mindset.

With this in mind, we can use influence as a principle of persuasion to persuade a prospective client or customer to buy a particular product or service. Equally, we can influence them to act or behave in a certain way if we were to show them that by not doing so would be inconsistent with their previous actions or behaviours.

If you want to influence somebody to develop a certain behaviour, you should first encourage them to exhibit that behaviour in a minor way. An example of this may be to encourage people to make small, concessionary commitments (such as signing a petition). By doing so, it becomes more likely that they will change their behaviour over time to remain consistent with these initial minor commitments. This will lead to a domino effect. It will become easier to influence each subsequent action or behaviour by increasing their level of engagement and commitment at each step. If you were to adhere to this process, it would ensure that the final domino (and your goal) will be toppled, with the final domino (or request) being much greater than the first.

When combined with the reciprocity principle of persuasion, consistency is an extremely potent behaviour to leverage to gain influence. One example of this would be if you are an online business. You may want to encourage someone to complete their name and address on an online contact form in order to receive a free gift or sample (reciprocity); this will make them far more likely to buy something from you further down the line (consistency).

When people are asked to do something for us, or more specifically to help us, they want to stay true to their word. In 1972, psychologist Thomas Moriarty conducted an experiment on Jones Beach in America[3]. When one of his team left a radio unattended on a beach blanket and another of his researchers, posing as a thief, stole it, he found that only 1 in 5 beach visitors intervened. However, in the second experiment, when the owner of the radio asked his neighbours on the beach to keep an eye on his belongings whilst he went for a swim, these people intervened 95% of the time, becoming near vigilantes, with some even chasing down the thief to retrieve the radio and preserve their word that they wanted to stay true to.

The desire for consistency within our lives is innate in all of us. It makes our lives simpler. Without the need to respond to each decision, most people place themselves on auto-pilot, allowing them time to focus on more important decisions. Steve Jobs and Mark Zuckerberg are perfect examples of this, wearing the same style of clothes each day, thus alleviating the need to decide what to wear each day, allowing them to focus on the more important decisions.

LIKEABILITY

Likeability is perhaps one of the most under-rated, under-estimated and least spoken about principles of persuasion. This is perhaps because everyone believes they are likeable. Yet, we have all seen those who have 'magnetic personalities' or are referred to as a 'people person'. You can bet they are having a greater impact and influence over the lives of others compared to those who don't have those traits. Essentially, people prefer to say "yes!" to people they like. There is a saying that "All things being equal, people like to do business with those they know, like and trust". Whilst I am in agreement with this, it's not 100% correct because people still do business with others when things aren't equal, and perhaps their product is more expensive or not quite as reliable as its competitors. Likeability, therefore, plays an overriding decision when it comes to considering those other factors. One of the main focuses for being likeable is that of authenticity. If you genuinely want to help your prospect overcome the problem surrounding the issue they are having with your product or service, and you can demonstrate that you care, are reliable, capable, and trustworthy in an authentic way, then this will foster a mutual relationship of likeability.

One of the most powerful applications to create likeability is the likeability formula. This allows you to convey to the customer that you have heard them, and you can empathise. One of the strongest ways to communicate this is to tell them about someone else who felt the same way as they did initially. The verbs you would use in this formula, and its application is below:

Feel + Felt + Found = Empathy (Creates greater influence)

This same formula can also be used for handling resistance in a sales situation and is interchangeable with building rapport or creating likeability.

If you were to place this into sentences, they could be applied like this:

1. I know how you feel
2. I felt the same way when
3. What I felt was

In one of my influence and sales training sessions I delivered in America recently, this was one of the replies we curated in response to an issue one of the delegates was having:

"I know how you feel. (1) Thanks for being so honest about the struggles you are having with your team. If I was in your shoes, I'd probably feel the exact same way. (2) I was speaking with another client (3) the other week that, funnily enough, was in a very similar position to you. We realized that their team was not being empowered enough, and certain members of their team were keen to develop into managerial roles. They had low employee satisfaction and high staff turnover. After some discussion, we identified the type of people that were leaving and their reasons and identified the team members who had the ambition to gain more authority.

We created some personal development plans, restructured some of the days for training, and looked at rotas to identify when they could gain hands-on team leader responsibility. We set up timelines and looked at opportunities around the business for them to work towards. Their feedback since then is that their branch has become a flagship for the other stores in terms of people development; they have coached several team members into full-time team leader roles, lowered their turnover, increased staff retention, and increased sales. If I could show you how this solution could be applied in your team and could save you far more than the cost of recruiting new staff and increasing your sales – would budget still be an issue?"

Here we applied the 'feel, felt found' formula. By cross-referencing the sentences, the first statement allows us to communicate similarity and empathy whilst the second delivers a compliment. When we communicate 'what we felt,' this also communicates another degree of similarity. The final sentence communicates a shared goal as is a perfect example of objection handling before any objection is presented.

To emphasise the importance of likeability, we turn to Joe Girard, an American Chevrolet car salesman who sold 13,001 cars between 1963 and 1978 and has been featured in the Guinness Book of Records as the seller of the most cars in a year (1,425 in 1973). Girard attributed three things to his success. First, he sold more than just the car. If any of his customers returned for a service, he would prioritize them and have 3 to 4 mechanics work on their car and even pay for some of the parts. In return, he simply asked them to come back. Secondly, and perhaps most famously, he sent each one of his customers a personalised card every month. He commissioned an artist to create a new design every month, and inside, he simply put "I like you". (Also triggering the principle of reciprocity) Similarly, he used this principle of reciprocity to take his employees out to dinner once a month. Without him requesting, they would work harder, which would result in repeat customers coming back. Girard's third approach to influence was that he was a regular guy. He didn't dress with expensive tastes, which made him much more relatable. People generally want to work for or alongside people who are similar. This final approach activates the consensus principle of persuasion.

In 2017, another Chevrolet salesman, Ali Reda, eclipsed Joe Girard's record of selling the highest number of cars in a year, and the secrets to his success are no different. His long term friend and coach said this:

"The business of your business is people. The key to massive success is to build and maintain meaningful, personal life long relationships. Do that, and you'll be profitable and proud." Damian Boudreaux

In his own words, Ali Reda said, "It's not about me". One of the fundamental keys to likeability is putting the other person first and being as interested in them as they are about you.

CONSENSUS / SOCIAL PROOF

Instead of trying to influence people by yourself, it can be wholly more effective to point to what many others are already doing or have already bought or done.

Many of us want to conform to societal norms and 'fit in with what most people do' and do 'what should be done', despite our belief we are individual. If enough people are doing something, we see this as acceptable and appropriate behaviour for us too, and psychologists have demonstrated this time and time again. When people are unsure of what to do, they look to others to influence their actions, reassure their behaviours, and then they follow suit accordingly. We do this to adapt to the world around us and help us to survive in a world full of different personalities and types of people.

We laugh at jokes on sitcoms (which may not be all that funny) because a laughter track has been placed over it, or we donate money into a basket of coins because we see that some coins are already in the basket. Equally so, we don't dig up someone else's flowers in their front garden for our own. These examples demonstrate how we adhere to social norms and consensus to fit into society and follow other people's leads.

Take social media as an example. If we are looking for a particular product or service, we may turn to online reviews. If we find that one product or service has 100 likes and the other has 20 likes, then most people would be more inclined to buy the item that more people have purchased. However, if you then realised that of the 20 likes of the other item, the majority were your friends, then you would be more inclined to buy that product or service instead. We are constantly searching for clues and cues to check the reliability and validity of the world around us and are more naturally disposed to believe things that other people believe is true.

For the sake of completeness, it is also worth considering the so-called false consensus effect. If we endorse products or services simply because other people have done so, simply to preserve our own prestige and reputation, then this can create a form of naïve realism. The inevitable consequence of this would be a reduced sensitivity to the notion that the reality may be very different to how it is actually presented. Life in society requires consensus as an indispensable condition.

For consensus to be valid, each individual should contribute independently out of his or her experience and insight. Coupled with social pressures and the ever-increasing need to fit in, which has been perpetuated by social media, this allows us to use consensus to persuade others to great success. This is especially true when your band, product or service has been endorsed by an authoritative source. This could come in the form of a person, the newspapers, TV or any respected publications or websites. If the source of this social proof is valid, reliable, and credible, then leveraging consensus into your influence strategy is very powerful indeed. From a business and sales perspective, research has shown that introductions to new clients or customers are worth 15 times as much profit compared to a cold call.

Consensus has been a powerful form of persuasion or method of influence throughout history, both intentionally and unintentionally. This has led to names such as The Werther Effect, mass shooting contagion, copycat crime, or copycat suicide as being synonymous with the unintentional influence of widely publicised tragic events. Celebrities or people who we see as similar to ourselves or we aspire to be can massively influence our choices.

Take copycat suicide as an example. When Marilyn Monroe committed suicide in 1962, at the beginning of August, her death was followed by an increase of 200 more suicides than average for that same month. A sudden increase of emulation suicides after a widely publicised suicide is also known as the Werther Effect

A copycat crime is another term synonymous with consensus. These crimes are usually inspired or modelled on a previous crime, and the term was first coined in 1916 due to the number of crimes that were committed in a similar style to Jack the Ripper.

Finally, extensive media coverage of mass shootings has also influenced copycat behaviour. This is particularly apparent in recent years. At the time in 1999, The Columbine School shooting was a one-off tragic event in history. However, since then, we have seen many mimicked mass shootings. A study conducted in 2015 suggests that the Columbine shooters have inspired a minimum of 21 mimicked shootings and 53 attempted plans to commit such an act in the U.S. over a 15 year period.[4]

Whilst consensus is generally leveraged to influence people to physically take action; it can be equally effective to persuade people not to take action[5]. In 2010, a proactive election campaign was launched in Trinidad and Tobago to suppress certain voters from going to the polls.

There were two main political parties in contention for leadership. One party was predominantly black, and the other, predominantly Indian. The People's Partnership Coalition election campaign was focused on targeting the youth, and in particular, first-time voters. Specifically, they wanted to increase the level of apathy from the youth through a campaign that was reactive and non-political because the youth did not care about politics.

The campaign team devised a campaign to be focussed around 'joining a gang', where they can be part of a movement and do something cool collectively. By focussing their campaign in this way, it was possible to create a consensus without being overly political. They created a 'Do So!' slogan which meant 'Do so, don't vote'. This partnered with a logo of crossed fists indicating a stance of resistance against politics and voting that could equally be mimicked in person.

This powerful message became a craze, and the youth were making viral YouTube videos and coming together as one. All of this began to snowball through the power of consensus. The campaign felt like it was an organic resistance or movement created by the youth, but it had, in fact, been instigated from the outset by the People's Partnership campaign team. Whilst even the Indian youth had fun joining in with the campaign, when the voting day finally arrived, they were not going to go against their parent's wishes. Instead of not voting, they did so. As a result of this apathy and an election campaign that encouraged large swathes of Trinidad and Tobago not to vote, this swung the election by 6% in favour of the People's

Partnership Coalition and resulted in Trinidad and Tobago's first-ever female Prime Minister.

This success was the result of an influential campaign encouraging apathy and targeting the emotions of the youth, not to take action collectively. The power of consensus-driven influence resulted in only 40% of 18-35-year-olds voting!

CONFIRMATION BIAS

When you make a concerted effort to influence someone using the principles mentioned previously, another consideration to take into account is that of 'confirmation bias'. It's human nature to cling to the belief that we are highly individual and our choices are our own. However, having worked in the field of influence and persuasion most of my life, I can say with certainty that one of the most predictable things about people is the fact that they believe they are unpredictable, which by default makes them more predictable.

Our belief is clouded by 'Confirmation Bias'. This is our tendency to gravitate towards information that confirms our current existing beliefs or ideas. In fact, Warren Buffet once said:

"What the human being is best at doing is interpreting all new information so that their prior conclusions remain intact."

Our rigidity or reluctance to evaluate any new information that contrasts with our current beliefs run deeper than just arrogance or loftiness, which it can sometimes be mistakenly interpreted as. Disseminating new evidence, especially when it's complicated or unclear, requires a great deal of mental energy. Constantly evaluating the worldview is quite frankly mentally exhausting. As a mental shortcut to make our lives easier, we prefer to strengthen our worldview based on our current beliefs and ideologies.

When considering confirmation bias and its relationship to influence, this can help shape our persuasion strategy. If we were to create our initial strategy using the OCEAN 5-personality trait, we might begin by asking our target audience some basic questions to help inform the advertising model we will adopt. However, questioning people about their personality can expose a flaw in these tests and equally highlight our confirmation bias.

One experiment conducted by Miriam Trope and Yacov Bassok[6] in 1983 evaluated the impact of 'confirmation bias' in a lab setting. Here, the researchers invited a selection of participants into their lab and split them into two groups.

One group was told the test subject was an extrovert, whilst the other was told they were an introvert. They were then told they can only ask questions that require a yes or no answer (except 'are you an extrovert' or 'are you an introvert' respectively), but could essentially ask any question but were not told the purpose of the experiment.

The test subject, on the other hand, is told to answer yes to everything.

At the end of the experiment, the participants made an assessment based on their answers as to whether the test subject was an extrovert or introvert. The group that was told the test subject was an extrovert believed they were, and the group who were told they were an introvert were just as convinced. This phenomenon arises because we only tend to ask questions that will confirm our suspicions or bias.

Let's conduct a similar experiment now – this is one for you to play along with. This experiment is known as the Wason Selection Task.

Imagine there are three A4 pieces of card. You look down and see the following:

On the first card, there is a picture of a teddy bear

On the second card, there is a picture of a boat

On the third card is the number 3

On the fourth card is the number 7

You are now furnished with the following piece of information, **which may be true or false**:

If there is a picture of a teddy bear on the front of one piece of card, then there is a number 3 on the other side.

With that information at hand, you must now decide which of the four cards you would turn over to confirm whether that rule is true or not?

Genuinely, make your choice.

Most people will say that they would either turn over the card with a picture of a teddy bear on the front or the card with the number 3 on it. However, they'd be wrong.

If there is a picture of a teddy bear on the front of one piece of card, then you have been told there is a number 3 on the other side. So, it makes sense to turn over the picture of the teddy bear to see if there is a number 3 staring back at us on the other side for confirmation.

However:

We would also have to turn over the card that has the number 7 on the front to see if the rule applied there too. If there is a picture of the teddy bear on the other side of the number 7, then the initial statement would be false. (Because if there is the picture of the teddy bear on the other side of the number 7, and not just the number 3, if on that one at all.)

Turning over the card with the number 3 on the front would not help us, as the statement does not say that if there is a three on one side, there should be a teddy bear on the other side. (It only states that if there is a bear on one side, there is a number 3 on the other side) In other words, if there was a picture of a boat or a teddy bear on the other side of the number 3, it would neither prove nor disprove the original statement. Thus, the correct answer would be to turn over the number 7.

The reason most people choose to turn over the card with the teddy bear on the front is due to confirmation bias, in that people generally look for things to confirm and not for things to disprove what they've been told. They want to see if the teddy bear has a number 3 on its reverse side or if the number 3 has a teddy bear on its reverse side. They don't think of trying to disprove the rule by seeing if there is a different number to the three on one side and the teddy bear on the reverse.

Similar to the preceding experiment, the participants try and prove that their test subject is an extrovert if they have been given a profile detailing them as an extrovert as opposed to trying to disprove they are an extrovert and vice versa when they have been told they are an introvert.

Neil de Grasse Tyson, the American astrophysicist, author, and science communicator, suggests that:

"One of the biggest problems with the world today is that we have large

groups of people who will accept whatever they hear on the grapevine, just because it suits their worldview—not because it is actually true or because they have evidence to support it. The striking thing is that it would not take much effort to establish validity in most of these cases, but people prefer reassurance to research."

With that in mind, if, as influencers, we accept our target audiences' world view (whether we agree with it or not) and take the key elements of the O.C.E.A.N personality model, combined with their demographic, geographic, and attitudinal characteristics, we can still distil down the things which support their world view and influence them accordingly. If we are able to acknowledge their core beliefs but not try to change or influence their belief structure, with the correct communication or advertising approach, we can influence this group too.

Perhaps the most contentious issue related to confirmation bias can be seen in conflicting arguments made between 'creationists' and 'evolutionary biologists'. Creationists place their belief in the accuracy of the bible and faith that earth is only a few thousand years old, with man created by Adam and Eve. Evolutionary biologists, however, use scientific evidence and empirical research to demonstrate how we have biologically evolved through millions of years, and the universe was created with the big bang. Creationists are aplomb at sidestepping the more scientific facts that disprove their ideas as it does not support their belief model. Whilst evolutionary biologists and anthropologists have used fossils to prove the process of evolution, creationists argue that these are proof of the global flood described in the bible or planted by God to test our belief.

For both sides, this confirmation bias eventually manifests itself in circular reasoning or, in other words, 'the fallacy of the true believer'. A 'true believer' dismisses any evidence that contradicts their belief system. Instead, they agree with everything that does. They hold onto these beliefs so tightly that it becomes a part of their identity. When a true believer finds others who reaffirm their view of the world, this can give rise to the creation of cults or mass movements.

Armed with the understanding that we pay more attention to things that confirm our existing beliefs than those that don't, we can finesse our advertising and marketing strategy or persuasive reasoning to align with this firmly held belief to make us more effective.

HEURISTICS

Humans like to avoid thinking about how they should react by using predictable shortcuts to guide their decisions. Advertisers take advantage of these pre-programmed human reactions and elicit a response that is in line with their advertising goal. They apply the fundamental principles of persuasion, including reciprocation, social proof, liking, authority, scarcity, and consistency, to influence our decisions.

To give an example of heuristics, Kevin Dutton poses a similar question to the one below in his superb book 'Flipnosois'[7]; I'd like you to imagine your friend has just bought a lottery ticket. They have chosen numbers 1,2,3,4,5,6 as their potentially winning numbers. Sadly, they didn't win; however, based on their ticket, which of the following winning sequences of numbers would give you the most amusement?

7, 8, 9, 10, 11, 12

OR

4, 14, 22, 33, 40, 45

If you chose one over the other, then this is heuristics at work. The lines of numbers have equal odds of coming out of the lottery machine regardless of their numerical sequence.

Kevin also poses another question:[8]

Imagine you have received an application form from somebody who has ticked a box saying that they are 6 foot 5 inches. The closer you look; you can't work out whether this second tick as to his profession is next to 'basketball player' or 'banker'. Which one is more likely?

If you said basketball player, then congratulations, you have chosen the same answer as 78% of Cambridge undergraduates. Unfortunately, similar to the Cambridge undergraduates, you are also incorrect.

Let say there are 100 basketball players and 5,000 bankers, proportionately speaking. Let's say 80% of basketball players are 6 foot five or taller; that's the equivalent of 80 players. In comparison, let's assume an extremely conservative 2% of bankers are 6 foot five or over. That equates to 100 bankers.

These two examples are of heuristics-in-action or otherwise known as 'mental shortcuts'. In these situations, our brain takes the incoming information and, based on probability and associations, makes a considered choice virtually subconsciously.

With the brain making hundreds of decisions a minute, to conserve its power, we rely on these mental shortcuts (or heuristics), so when the need comes to make an important decision to preserve our health and wellbeing, for example, it is a lot more agile and can react much faster.

People are subconsciously applying these heuristics to everyday situations, but this corner-cutting can also result in errors or misguided judgments of a situation.

In a world where we are being exposed to more and more

information at every minute of the day, certainly through social media or online news, advertisers have to think more creatively to communicate their persuasive messages to us. Research from a UK attention technology company, 'Lumen research' has found that only 4% of digital ads get more than 1 second of attention whilst only 1/5 of all ads get looked at all. With these striking statistics to consider, it is no wonder why creative agencies are curating clickbait headlines to attract our attention. These are often simple and compelling messages with curiosity hooks built-in and are designed to capture our attention amongst the rest of the 'online noise'.

As people become more inoculated against clickbait-style headers and adverts and as the number of websites on the World Wide Web gets larger, it's becoming increasingly important to consider your content more carefully. From an engagement perspective, as the technology progresses at an ever-increasing rate and attention rates are going down, readers, viewer's or prospective clients are relying more and more on heuristics or mental shortcuts to inform their decisions.[9]

Persuasive messages can still be used to influence consumers into buying a particular product or service through the exploitation of social heuristics. In 2003, researcher J. Sean McCleneghan studied two prominent women's magazines.[10] His research found that in a sample of Cosmopolitan and Glamour magazines sold, the word 'sex' appeared in more than 46% of the 186 headlines. Furthermore, 62% of the headlines implied 'sex' with phrases such as 'erotic tastes,' 'intimate affairs,' and more. This was supported by additional content analysis and Likert scale measurements to determine 23 attitudinal statements. Whilst it is neither subtle, sophisticated, nor refined, the old adage of 'sex sells' still rings true. Sex, when employed as a curiosity hook, is another example of a heuristic shortcut that both Cosmopolitan and Glamour magazines exploited to sell their latest editions. Alongside sexuality, freedom, and opportunity also featured heavily in the headlines and content to encourage women to buy.

As well as sex, scare stories, fear, scarcity, time restrictions, and excitement, or other factors which generate a strong emotive response can also trigger mental shortcuts and should be considered when curating a persuasive ad or influencing people to change their actions or behaviours. If this is applied to groups, teams, societies, or larger organizations, this can trigger the consensus principle of persuasion and lead to stereotyped thinking – another powerful form of influence.

FIXED BEHAVIOUR PATTERNS

During the mating season, the stickleback fish displays an amazing pattern of behaviour. First, its belly turns red and attacks other males (also exhibiting a red belly). In the same season, it also tries to mate with female sticklebacks that have a plump belly. What makes this incredible is that even in a simulated environment using a crude model of a stickleback with a red belly, the fish will still attack it, and if another stickleback model is used with a plump belly, it will still try and mate with it.

A similar phenomenon can be seen in female turkeys. They display all the roles of a good mother turkey - preparing the nest, feeding their young, and protecting their offspring underneath their wing. This mothering is triggered by the 'cheep-cheep' sound that their offspring emits. Unusually for a female turkey, the more traditional stimuli to recognize their young such as smell, touch, and appearance, play a much less significant role.

Researchers found that these sounds are so influential on the female turkey's decision to mother their young that even when they put a device that emitted a replicated 'cheep-cheep' sound of their young inside a cuddly polecat toy, the female turkey is still happy to take this under her wing and mother it. Even more surprising is that the polecat is a natural enemy to a turkey which the turkey would avoid under any other circumstances. This was demonstrated when the sound emitter was switched off, and the turkey viciously switched from nurturing the cuddly toy to viciously attacking it.

There are many other examples of these unusual behaviours in the animal kingdom and are often referred to as Fixed Behaviour Patterns (F.B.Ps). They show no logic or conscious thought processes. It led me to question if Fixed Behaviour Patterns are also exhibited in humans and, if so, can they be leveraged to give us an influential edge.

Despite everyone having a strong sense of identity and proud of their individuality, As I mentioned earlier, I've found through years of working with people both on and off-stage in countless countries, one of the most predictable things about people is the fact that they believe they are unpredictable. This in itself makes them more predictable.

To give you an example, in my keynote presentations, masterclasses or performances, I perform a demonstration in which somebody would think of an object, and I use my skillset to pick up on clues and cues to identify what object that person is thinking of. Sometimes a gentleman comes onto the stage that portrays the image of a 'wannabee' alpha male. Occasionally, this demeanour is accompanied by the phrase *'you'll never guess what I'm thinking'*. He has now presented himself as a challenge and will follow this up by keeping a poker face and as motionless as possible. With over 15 years of working with people and the principles of persuasion, he is only going to think one of two things, and both of them are going to be rude.

Here, the gentleman in question believes he has a completely free choice to think of anything he wants. In fact, he does, but he doesn't think that I would think that he would think of one of those things, and thus, his fixed behaviour pattern kicks in to try and 'catch me out' and retreats into his own mind without taking advantage of the creative freedom he has been given.

I could equally ask somebody to think of a number between 1 and 10, and 90% of the time, they will choose the number 7. If I was to ask a lady to think of a playing card, they would more than likely choose the 7 of hearts or Queen of hearts. Men, on the other hand, gravitate more towards the ace of spades.

The question still remains - is it possible to influence somebody or at the very least modify their behaviour to generate a Fixed Behaviour Pattern?

After some thought, I realized that we all exhibit these Fixed Behaviour Patterns in our everyday life.

Perhaps we find ourselves going out to a new restaurant and the last time you went out you tried a new dish that you hadn't had before, but saw it again on this menu. There is a high chance you will order this again despite not knowing if it will taste the same as you enjoyed it last time.

Equally, we may buy VIP tickets to go and see the sequel to a movie we watched recently. We thought the first one was enjoyable, but there is no telling if the next one will be, as there are no reviews to help us decide.

The same can be said if a comedian releases new tour dates. There's no way of knowing what material they will be sharing and whether it will be as funny as last time, but despite this lack of knowledge, ticket offices sell out within hours.

Another fixed behaviour pattern is based on the belief that 'price indicates quality'. However, as we will read later, this is merely an assumption and can often be incorrect. In fact, souvenir shops in London raise the prices of unpopular lines to give them the appeal of being in demand or having high quality. Shoppers then allow their Fixed Behaviour Patterns to influence their next purchase and end up buying several unpopular lines.

Fixed Behaviour Patterns can also be seen in physical actions. When researching this book, I delved deeper into the application of mirroring. Mirroring is the behavior that one person unconsciously imitates from another.

Generally, if we nod, there is an increased tendency for the person we are sat opposite to nod in agreement. These Fixed Behaviour Patterns can be seen in even greater technicolour when we yawn. If we genuinely yawn or simulate a yawn, regardless of its authenticity, we will find that those around us will also start yawning too. Applied to the business arena, nodding, smiling, flattery, and a gentle massaging of the prospective clients' ego all elicit a positive Fixed Behaviour Pattern, which, if delivered authentically, will result in a positive response.

INFLUENCE WITHOUT AWARENESS

One of the most exciting parts about my job is that the techniques, principles, and applications that I share in my keynotes or corporate consulting encourages us to question our own 'free will'. Some of my greatest successes delivering these programs or masterclasses have been encouraging delegates to achieve a shift in both their own perception and understanding how prospective customers think

One of the most fundamental parts of being a successful persuader or influencer is to remain authentic. A lack of authenticity is easy to spot and soon renders any negotiation worthless if the prospective client thinks you are trying to manipulate them with sneaky tactics. As a result, your ability to influence or persuade is most effective when the target is not even aware of it. I call it 'Influence without Awareness'.

In its most basic form James Vicary, a market researcher best known for pioneering the concept of subliminal advertising, conducted an experiment in 1957 to explore the idea of influence without awareness. He wanted to see if he could influence theatre goers' actions and behaviours by flashing commands on the screen so quickly, they would not consciously see the messages and only register them subconsciously. He believed that by using phrases such as "Hungry, eat popcorn" or "Thirsty, drink Coca-Cola", he could influence them to eat and drink more of those products, respectively.

Vicary claimed that this technique saw sales of both popcorn and coca-cola rise by 57% and 18%, respectively. That same year, journalist Vance Packard supported these claims in his book "Hidden Persuaders," which led to a public outcry and banning of subliminal messages, suggesting they were manipulative.

A few years later, in 1962, Vicary admitted that he had never conducted the subliminal "experiment" — and he devised it as a gimmick to attract customers to his failing marketing business. However, this term had been coined, and in 1973, this term brought rise to a book called Subliminal Seduction by Wilson Bryan Key, where he cited specific examples from Playboy, Vogue, and Cosmopolitan magazines, which demonstrated the ways in which the media uses sex and violence to manipulate human actions and behaviours. These kinds of techniques are more in line with subliminal messaging, which is more covert and manipulative. Authentic influence without awareness presents a much more ethical approach to influencing others, unlike these aforementioned subliminal messages, which were invisible and used covertly.

Persuading or influencing others should be authentic, and your consideration for others should be just as high as your own. If applied correctly and effectively, influence without awareness could be likened to yawning when some else yawns or whistling a tune that you don't know why you are whistling until you really look back over the day to realize it was being piped through the loudspeaker in a shop.

THE EXPERIMENTS

The following experiments have been hand-picked to demonstrate a wide range of ideas behind the art of influence. I have mixed some of the classics in behavioural psychology with more recent studies as well as some more obscure studies. I'll begin each experiment by posing a question linked to the experiment to give you the opportunity to decide what you would do. Think of it from your perspective and then take into account the principles of persuasion, ideas and concepts shared earlier.

Although the following experiments won't give you the opportunity to partake in person in the same environment that was tested, I sincerely hope it allows you to consider your choices, actions, or behaviour before reading the associated experiment. Regardless of your answer, the experiments and subsequent analysis will either support your current skill-set or give you new insights, thoughts, or ideas to apply in your own life. Taking part in the following experiments allows you to be the scientist, researcher, and participant all in one. I'll add a little footnote after each experiment to outline which persuasion of influence principles or ideas were at play.

I have cherry-picked the most eye-opening experiments conducted where the results and revelations say something about the choices we make or don't make in relation to influence or persuasion. These experiments were conducted by some of the world's most revered psychologists. These range from Cialdini to Skinner and from Milgram to Asch. You'll also experience experiments by some of today's modern psychologists, from Wiseman to Ariely and Barrett to Diehl.

Much like these modern-day researchers and psychologists, I hope that this book breathes new life into your understanding of human psychology and your understanding and application of influence both at work and in your private life. You can even try some of these experiments out on your friends, devise new ones, or simply use them to encourage amazing dinner party debates and discussions, giving you more authority and making you more likeable! Enjoy.

EXPERIMENT 1

The question:

Does a beautiful person hold more influence over people than somebody less attractive?

The experiment:

In 1972, researchers Dion, Berschield, and Walster showed 100 yearbook photographs to a select group of college students. [11] The students were asked to rate the attractiveness of each of them as either very high (attractive), ordinary (average level of attractiveness), or low (unattractive). Once these photos had been split into their subsection, a new group of students was asked to cast their eyes over the new piles. They were asked what qualities they would give to the people in the three piles. They could describe them as kind, altruistic, warm, trustworthy, deceitful, etc.

Would you label an attractive person with a more positive personality trait label than a negative one?

YES / NO

If you said yes, your answer is in line with the student participants. They gave the people who had been deemed as attractive in the photographs more positive traits and the people in the photographs who were deemed as less attractive more negative qualities.

Principles of persuasion at work:

This, of course, follows the likeability principle of persuasion. Our society is becoming increasingly obsessed with the image it portrays to the world. Certainly, this has become more apparent since the advent of social media, and we have become increasingly obsessed with the beauty of ourselves and of others. We may follow brands or people who display very few positive traits other than their beautiful looks. Whilst beauty and looks can help us influence others, a brand, company, or online influencer is more successful if they also communicate other positive traits.

EXPERIMENT 2

The question:

Which one is the correct answer?

The experiment:

Below, you can see two images. The image on the left represents the reference line whilst the image on the right represents the comparison lines. You are not allowed to use a ruler or any other form of measuring device. This is not an eyesight test. You will play the role of the 9th participant, similar to the original experiment. As in the original experiment, you will hear from the other participants first as to which of the three lines A, B, or C is the same length as the single line on the left. I cannot tell you any more information about the participants.

Participant 1 thinks the answer is A

Participant 2 thinks the answer is B

Participant 3 thinks the answer is B

Participant 4 thinks the answer is A

Participant 5 thinks the answer is C

Participant 6 thinks the answer is A

Participant 7 thinks the answer is B

Participant 8 thinks the answer is A

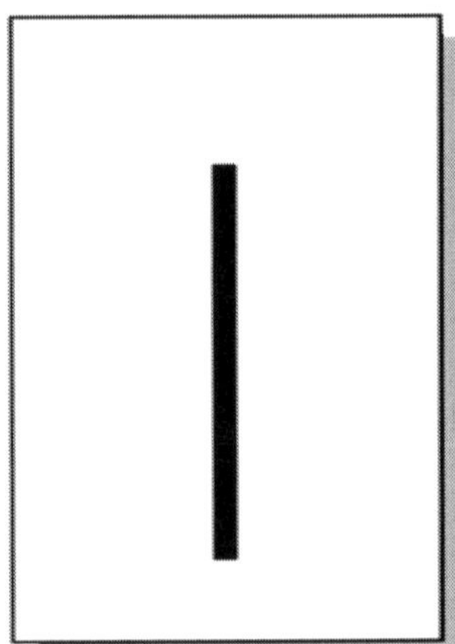

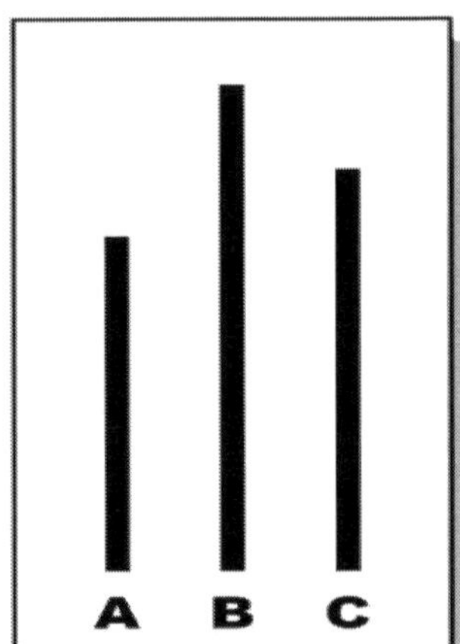

With that in mind, which of the following lines A, B or C, is the same length as the reference line?

A / B / C

Principles of persuasion at work:

The answer here is C. Consensus is the principle of persuasion at work here. In 1962, psychologist Solomon Ash wanted to put this principle of persuasion to the test and see if we really do what other people do, to the extent where we would even doubt our own eyes and our own sense of reality.[12] The experiment described above is how it played out except for one fundamental difference. The other participants were actually stooges and had been briefed prior to the experiment to give specific answers – the incorrect ones (with one genuine answer to add a little bit of validity).

In the actual experiment, the (stooged) research assistants were asked to share their pre-planned choice with the other participant (who, in this case, was you). The true participant in the subject was not briefed that this was happening, of course, and despite the real test subject totally disbelieving the answers of the other participants (stooges), over several tests, they invariably chose the most popular line that the stooges had said.

In fact, over a third of the genuine participants went with one of the incorrect answers being given by the stooges. Over the 12 repeated experiments, about 75% of participants conformed at least once, and approximately 25% of participants never conformed. When there was no influence from stooges, less than 1% of the participants gave the incorrect answer. This emphasizes the power of consensus and how it can influence people to make a choice that goes against their beliefs and even their own sense of reality.

Applied to the sales arena, and in specific examples like an auction, we get caught up in the moment if we see other people buying the same thing that we want. We even feel even more influenced to do what others are doing or buy what others are buying. This is also known as 'emotional contagion'. However, the power of consensus is perhaps the most vulnerable principle of persuasion to losing its effectiveness quickly. If one person in the group does not agree with the opinions and views of the rest of the group, who collectively have differing opinions or views, then this can quickly result in an uprising or rebellion. This is more likely to happen if others in the group are thinking but not sharing their concerns or difference of opinions as they are fearful of not conforming themselves. As a result, it's important not to confuse other people's inaction or silence as agreement.

EXPERIMENT 3

The question:

Above your normal tipping quota (if you don't tip, shame on you, but use that as your benchmark), how much extra would you tip the waiter if they added a fun puzzle on your bill?

The experiment:

You've been out for a meal. The food and drink have been fantastic and the service equally good. You, your belly, and your friends are satisfied. The waiter then presents you the bill, and on it is a little game for you to play before you pay. It asks you to count the number of Fs within the following sentence:

FINISHED FILES ARE THE RESULT OF YEARS OF SCIENTIFIC STUDY COMBINED WITH THE EXPERIENCE OF MANY YEARS

You can do this too. How many Fs are there?

Whilst this behavioural psychology experiment is more than just this puzzle - I hope many of you will feel a dry smile come over your face when I tell you that there are, in fact, six Fs. Did you guess six? If so, well done! Most people guess three. The reason most people say three is because they verbalize the sentence and intonate the 'Fs' as a 'V,' thus miscounting. Whilst I admit it might not be the most fun puzzle you ever had the pleasure to undertake – if your answer was three, but now that I've told you the correct answer is 6, I'm hoping it's made you smile.

Now back to the bill and the restaurant. You've had a go with the puzzle, and now you are about to pay and tip. The waiter has made you smile by telling you the correct answer is 6. Do you:

A. Tip the same as you always tip?
B. Does the puzzle frustrate you so much, so you don't give any tips?
C. Have you enjoyed this extra puzzle, and you tip a little bit more?

If you are similar to most of the participants who took part in this experiment, it should have made you smile, put you in a good mood, and as a result, you would have tipped the waiter a bit more. Conducted in 2001 by psychologists Bruce Rind and David Strohmetz, they printed this puzzle on some bills and not on others to act as a control group.[13] What they found was that after collecting the tips from both groups that the test group received on average 20% more tips than the control group!

For most people, participating in little puzzles and games are fun and puts us in a good mood, encouraging us to give a more generous tip. Studies have shown that this idea can be amplified even further by adding a smiley face or a cute drawing to the bill too.

Principles of persuasion at work:

This experiment takes advantage of the idea of reciprocity as a principle of persuasion. We have given a gift of a smile to the customer, in this case, through a little puzzle on their bill. This means that they are now somewhat indebted to repay that gift, albeit in a small way – in this case, in the form of a tip. This dovetails with the principle of likeability, and the two combined, influence the diners to give a higher tip.

EXPERIMENT 4

The question:

Let's suppose you were given a really, really boring task to undertake and had to do it for 1 hour. After you have completed this hour and were asked to give some feedback, would you change your answer depending on the amount you got paid? For example, if you only got paid £1, would your feedback about the boring job you have just done be more or less favourable compared to if you had been paid £20 (Of course, a feeling of indifference may be an option here, but if you were presented with just two options)?

MORE / LESS FAVOURABLE

The experiment:

Psychologists Leon Festinger and James Carlsmith carried out the following cognitive dissonance experiment in 1959.[14] In it, they gave 12 participants 12 spools of thread (without the thread on them) and asked them to put the spools on a tray, then take them off, then put them back on again. They performed this mundane task for 30 minutes. At the end of this, they were then placed in front of a board that had 48 pegs. For this next task, each participant had to turn each peg a quarter-turn clockwise. They had to do this with all 48 pegs. Once they had done this, they then had to start the process again, turning the first peg a quarter turn clockwise and so on and so forth, for a further 30 minutes. The job itself was not relevant to the experiment, but giving them a really mundane and boring task for them to complete for an hour, was.

At the end of the test, they were ushered into an adjacent room where the next participant was waiting. The researchers told them to tell the next participant that the task they had just completed was really interesting. Half of the test subjects were paid £1 to say this whilst the others were paid £20. This was then followed by a quick survey where they had to rate how interesting the activity was.

The researchers found that those who were paid £20 said the activity was really boring. In contrast, those who were paid a measly £1 said that that the activity wasn't that bad.

Principles of persuasion at work:

Festinger and Carlsmith had activated the consistency and authority principle of persuasion here and, in doing so, had influenced some of the participants to contradict themselves. They had all had a really boring experience, but because a researcher (in a position of authority) had told them to lie, they had simply done so. However, the more startling principle of persuasion demonstrated was that of consistency. Those who were paid £20 had a financial incentive, and therefore, an excuse for telling a lie. As a result, it didn't matter too much to them that they said one thing and did another. However, those who were paid just £1 felt less comfortable. They resolved this unease by convincing themselves that the task wasn't that bad after all. This uneasiness is what Festinger and Carlsmith have labelled "cognitive dissonance" and is caused by holding two conflicting beliefs, attitudes, or values.

As people generally have an innate desire to avoid this discomfort and we influence ourselves to behave a certain way despite the inconsistency with our actions. One example comes from people eating meat yet also considers themselves to be an animal lover and even dislikes the thought of killing animals. Other examples include people who smoke despite being aware of the adverse effects of tobacco, or even those buying a new car that is not fuel-efficient despite being environmentally conscious.

Cognitive dissonance and consistency are also apparent when people read the reviews of a product or service after they have purchased or used them. If they read a review that doesn't agree with their opinion, they may argue that the 'reviewer doesn't know what they're talking about. Others who write reviews about the same item or service will be regarded as 'having good common sense or a 'valid opinion'.

When we make these assumptions after making a purchase, this is called "post—decisional dissonance". Once you make a purchase, you agree with other people who share the same glowing reviews as you do but label those who contradict these positive reviews as 'wrong'. We want to remain consistent with the belief that we made the correct choice or decision in the first place.

Much like consensus with the outside world, we like to avoid conflict within ourselves as well. If our internal conflict is strong, then we 'bend' reality a bit and focus on the facts we agree with and disregard those that we don't.

EXPERIMENT 5

The question:

You are assessing applications for Graduate School. You can choose which applicant - A, B, or C to accept. Which one do you choose?

APPLICANT A

I want to go to Graduate School so that I can learn to know the literature well. I want to explore the shape and the meaning of the novel and its literary antecedents. I want to understand what the novel has meant in different literary periods and what it is likely to become. I want to explore its various forms, realism, naturalism, and other modes, and the Victorian and Modernist consciousness as they are revealed.

APPLICANT B

I want to go to Graduate School so that I can learn to recognize literature well. I want to explore the character and the meaning of the novel and its literary antecedents. I desire to understand what the novel has represented in different literary periods and what it is likely to become. I desire to explore its different manners, realism, naturalism and other modes, and the Victorian and Modernist consciousness as they are revealed.

APPLICANT C

I desire to go to Graduate School so that I can learn to recognize literature satisfactorily. I want to investigate the character and the connotation of the narrative and its literary antecedents. I desire to comprehend what the narrative has represented in numerous literary periods and what it is expected to become. I desire to investigate its numerous manners, realism, naturalism, and other approaches, and the Victorian and Modernist consciousness as they are discovered.

The experiment:

In 2006, a professor at Stanford University, Daniel Oppenheimer, conducted a study to examine the effect long words have on our impression of intelligence.[15] He used the paragraph belonging to Applicant A, above, as the original version, chosen from a selection of different essays written by college seniors as to why they wanted to go to graduate school for a degree in English Literature. He then proceeded to replace nouns, verbs, and adjectives to make the paragraph increasingly more complex. Participants read through the paragraphs as you have just done and then decided whether to accept the applicant into Graduate School or not and rate their level of confidence in making this decision. In the example above, applicant C received the fewest number of acceptances with the least amount of confidence placed in their decision, and the original application (applicant A) received the highest number of acceptances with the highest amount of confidence.

Oppenheimer also discovered that when the paragraphs were written in a font that was more difficult to read, the reader would perceive the author as less intelligent. As a result, you could potentially influence others to perceive you as more academically gifted by writing in a simpler font or typography and more simple sentence structures.

Principles of persuasion at work:

Einstein once said:

"If you can't explain it simply, you don't understand it well enough.

With that in mind, authority is the principle of persuasion alluded to in the experiment above. If you can communicate what you want to say clearly and succinctly, this telegraphs that you are an authority on your particular subject and can influence people to follow you, or in this case, choose you.

When applied to business, many businesses have websites that operate on the WordPress content management system. Perhaps the most popular plugin to assist with Search Engine Optimisation (how to tailor your website to perform higher in the listings on Google) is called Yoast SEO. Here they identify the 'Flesch reading score' as a contributing factor to where you would feature in Google's search engine results. This is by no means a deciding factor, but keeping your sentences short, simple, and easy to understand can improve the SEO (search engine optimization) of your website. A higher ranking website results in more traffic, which means more sales leads and potentially more profit.

EXPERIMENT 6

The question:

If you were an estate agent, do you think you would make more sales if you answered the phone to a prospective client and shared your own credentials or if one of your colleagues transferred the call to you, having shared your credentials with the prospective client first?

WHEN YOU ANSWER / WHEN THE CALL IS TRANSFERRED TO YOU

The experiment:

Behavioural psychologist, Robert Cialdini who we've met a couple of times in this book, was invited into a real estate agency to assist them with their sales techniques.[16] He was specifically requested to help them create more appointments and increase the number of contracts they signed with their clients.

As with many companies where the phone is the first point of contact with the agent, Cialdini and his team found that the colleagues in the agency were transferring calls to one another with standard scripts such as "Oh lettings, you need to speak to Sandra, let me put you through" or "You need the sales department. Let me connect you with Peter".

Cialdini and his team noticed that there was an opportunity to build authority as the principle of persuasion into the call. They also found that they could build this into the calls as they were being transferred, allowing any inferences to authority coming from a third party, which has more credibility. They tweaked the generic script to a more credential driven one:

"Oh lettings, you need to speak to Sandra, who has over 15 years of experience letting properties in this neighbourhood. Let me put you through now."

If the client wanted to find out more about selling or buying a house, the team would transfer the call to another agent using the script:

"I'm going to put you through to Peter, our head of sales. Peter has 20 years of experience selling properties. In fact, he recently sold a property very similar to yours."

Both of these revised scripts deliver authority to Sandra and Peter even before they speak to the client, and because these credentials have been communicated through a third party in the form of the transferring agent, they have no need to be boastful anymore. At the same time, the information shared is authentic, so the sales agents taking the call don't feel the need to over-inflate their credentials. By connecting to their best agents, it makes the prospective client feel like they are being looked after personally. Personalization in any interaction increases the influential leverage you may have over them too.

These minor changes cost the real estate agency nothing and required no extra work. However, with just a tweak in script and modification of the technique used to transfer calls, this resulted in a 20% rise in appointments and a 15% increase in the number of signed contracts.

Principles of persuasion at work:

The authority principle of persuasion is at work here. Authority is an even more powerful form of influence when communicated through a third party. People have a greater tendency to trust and obey authority figures which hark back to the younger years of our lives, mentioned earlier. We have been educated to obey authority such as teachers, religious leaders, the police, and newsreaders, and as such, we are heavily indoctrinated to follow their authority into adulthood too.

It is, however, our parents who we obey the wishes of even more than the professions above. When we were young, our parents were the main authority figures who we obeyed. It could be argued that we not only obey our parents out of respect but also from an evolutionary perspective – to survive. At the same time as nurturing us and instilling discipline within us, our parents also gave us food and shelter. It is logical to think that we associate one with the other, even if it just on a subconscious level. As a result, it could be argued that this commitment to obeying authority figures is to some extent evolutionary hard-wired into us and ensures that authority as a principle of persuasion remains as influential and powerful as ever.

EXPERIMENT 7

The question:

Which of the following group of questions and answers are your favourite – those in section A or B?

QUESTIONS A

1. What breed of dog is the only animal whose evidence is admissible in court? (A bloodhound)
2. What snack food is an ingredient in the explosive – dynamite? (Peanuts)
3. What is the only animal besides a human that can get sunburnt? (A Pig)

QUESTIONS B

1. Which sports athlete has appeared in McDonald's, Nike, and Haines advertisements? (Michael Jordan)
2. How long were Jerry Seinfeld and his friends sentenced in the series finale? (One year)
3. Which school has the most students over the age of twenty-five, according to U.S News? (University of Phoenix)

Remember your favourites.

The experiment:

In 2009, psychologists Min Jeong Kang et al. conducted a test to examine what happens to our brains when our curiosity is piqued.[17] Kang and his team selected several participants and put them through an MRI (magnetic resonance imaging) scanner individually. He asked a number of questions similar to the examples above to see if parts of their brain became more active if more 'high curiosity questions' were asked over 'low curiosity questions.'

The questions in section A are deemed to have a higher level of curiosity, whilst those in section B, which are deemed to have a lower level curiosity factor.

Kang and his team found that the parts of the brain that became most activated when the high curiosity questions were asked are more related to the reward and memory centres. This implies that the brain rewards us when we find out the answer to a difficult question, and the memory region of our brain kicks in to store that information.

Principles of persuasion at work:

Whilst greater knowledge gives us increased authority and thus more influence, we are naturally drawn to the questions which we think people wouldn't normally know. This curiosity in the answer activates the principle of scarcity within us in that we are drawn to something (the answer) we don't have.

We are the target of influence every day, with websites creating 'clickbait' titles that often have a 'curiosity element' built into them. In the world of internet marketing, if you click on something which has piqued your interest through curiosity, there's a high chance that your behaviour is being tracked, and you will then be marketed with similar products and services through pop-ups or more covert advertising.

In marketing and advertising, this persuasion technique is often referred to as 'creating curiosity hooks'. Of these, Russell Brunson, the CEO and founder of click funnels identifies 5 of these hooks

1.Little known big differences

This concept shows people something that they aren't aware of and how knowing more about it could make the difference between success and failure. This is why some online videos go viral – because they are cool and new. A new discovery of something can also increase your perceived status and, therefore, authority.

2.Well known little understood

This is a concept where you take something that everyone thinks they know about and show them that they are potentially sabotaging their success because they are missing certain nuances or details.

3. This changes everything

This idea is applicable if something new has happened in your prospect's market. This new development in their market is related to the problem your prospect wants to solve and highlights to them that if they aren't aware of it, they are at risk of missing out.

4.Crystal ball theory

This hook suggests that if something has been done successfully in the past, then there's a likelihood it is about to be made obsolete. Your hook will persuade them that this will soon be common knowledge, but if they get in now, they can have early success.

5.Revisiting the fundamentals

This final angle takes the approach that things are getting too complicated, sophisticated, or advanced for the average person. This is particularly relevant in some sectors of IT. You present them with the opportunity to take things back to basics without compromising functionality and efficiency.

EXPERIMENT 8

The question:

Would you be more motivated if you had a regular reward for your work or irregular rewards for your work?

REGULAR / IRREGULAR

The experiment:

One of the most influential 20th-century psychologists, B.F Skinner, conducted the following experiment in 1948, primarily to explore behaviourism and operant conditioning.[18] He would place various animals in a Skinner box and assess their responses to reward stimuli. For example, if he placed a pigeon in the box, and it would peck a key, then the pigeon would receive a reward, and so over time, the pigeon became conditioned to receive a reward for each time it pecked at a key. Skinner would even get them raising their heads as high as they could go or playing table tennis. He was able to condition all their behaviours by rewarding them with food.

He then went on to place the pigeon in the Skinner box without giving rewards for anything. No matter what the pigeon did, there would be no reward in the form of food. However, after this had been established, at random, the Skinner box would automatically deliver rewards. After a few hours, Skinner would return to find one pigeon turning round in circles, another pecking at the key, and another preening under its left-wing or scraping at the ground. Each pigeon had associated the reward with whatever action it was doing at the time and continued doing so in the hope it would receive another reward.

Skinner also performed his experiment with other animals such as rats too. He observed that once the rats became conditioned to receiving food pellets, their rate of activation would drop when they were not specifically seeking food. However, when Skinner altered the mechanism to provide random releases of food similar to the pigeons, the rate of activation increased.

Skinner theorized that the delivery of the inconsistent reward was, in fact, a greater motivator for action because the reward, while still desired, was not guaranteed with each repetition of the action.

Principles of persuasion at work:

The principle of persuasion at work here is the principle of reciprocity. People are generally more influenced when they feel indebted to someone who has given them something first. To give this principle even more, weight giving something unexpected (and personal) is often even more appreciated.

Skinner and other psychologists have looked at how the Skinner box results compare with our own outdated belief system. The actions of the pigeon, are in many ways, similar to how a tribe may sacrifice a goat in order to make it rain for the crops.

With a little creativity, you can use the results for your own influence experiments or sales techniques. The idea of 'shaping', which is evident in this experiment, is used in our society to help children to learn through positive reinforcement or help people to overcome their fears or phobias using similar techniques through the application of incremental changes.

EXPERIMENT 9

The question:

Is it possible to influence one group to hate another within the space of a day where the members of both groups don't initially know one another?

YES / NO

The experiment:

The answer to this question seems obvious, seeing as I asked it, and it is. However, the experiment which supports it is not only fascinating but adds some real value to our understanding of influence. In 1954, psychologist Muzafer Sherif conducted an experiment to study the positive and negative intergroup attitudes between experimentally produced groups.[19] This study has become more commonly known as the 'Robbers cave'. In it, Sherif took a group of psychologically stable 12-year-old boys, with their parents' consent to a park consisting of 200 acres of forest. Here, Sherif randomly separated the boys out into one of two groups and ensured that neither group knew of the existence of the other. Throughout the experiment, Sherif played the role of the park janitor whilst his research team posed as other members of the camp coordinators.

With the scene set, the children spent time hiking, playing baseball, and swimming in their respective groups. They collectively decided on the names of their groups as 'Rattlers' and 'Eagles'. On an agreed morning, the research team told the groups about the other's existence and then organized competitive games between the two of them, including tug-of-war and baseball, all accompanied with trophies and medals. These competitive activities soon sparked fierce competition, which led to name-calling, stealing from one another (instigated by the research team), and getting into fights with sticks and bats and socks filled with rocks.

Each group had created their own sense of identity. When the boys were interviewed at points during the experiment, each group described their own members as 'brave' and 'tough' and the members of the other team as 'sneaky' and 'untrustworthy'. Despite both teams going to Sunday religious services together on one of the days during the experiment, they still plotted to carry attacks on one another.

Sherif was also interested in examining whether he could encourage the boys to behave as a collective group and whether it was possible to bond them together just as easily as it was to instigate the rivalry. To identify this, his team intentionally damaged the water supply to the camp and informed both groups that some vandals had done it. Interestingly, despite their differences, both groups came together to restore the working condition of the water supply. Sherif expanded on this idea even further by pretending that the vehicle that was transporting both groups had broken down. Again they came together as a unit to help fix it and even sang collectively whilst one played the ukulele.

Principles of persuasion at work:

When people feel they have bonded with one another, much like the Rattlers and the Eagles did, they often act in unison. Consensus is the principle of persuasion at play here. We see similar behaviours to the Rattlers and Eagles in today's society in sporting events where supporters cheer for their favourite team or at political rallies where attendees applaud speeches.

One stone that remains left unturned is what principles of persuasion were used in the letters sent to the boy's parents who were involved in the experiment to encourage them to let their children spend time at an unknown camp with unknown people. Gina Perry, the author of the Lost Boys, suggests that the letters in question "are a lesson in the art of skillful deception and subtle persuasion".

EXPERIMENT 10

The question:

Imagine that the United States of America is preparing for the outbreak of a brand-new disease that is expected to kill 600 people. Two alternative programs to combat the disease have been proposed. Which program do you think most people would choose:

1. If program A is adopted, 200 people will be saved.
2. If program B is adopted, there is a 1/3 probability that 600 people will be saved and a 2/3 probability that no people will be saved.

Would you choose program A or B?

A / B

The experiment:

The question detailed above was the same one used in the experiment carried out in 1986 by Amos Tversky and Daniel Kahneman to explore rational choice and the framing of decisions.[20] Participants were posed the question above, and about 78% of them chose program A. The reasons they gave for making that choice was that it sounded better in terms of the number of people saved and also due to the simplicity of it. In reality, both programs, A and B, save the same number of people. This reaffirmed the researchers' suspicions that as humans, we don't often think through complicated decisions and are influenced more by what our attention is drawn to. Most people are risk-averse, meaning that we are more naturally drawn to the program, which is framed in the most straightforward way and appears to save the most lives.

Principles of persuasion at work:

The outcome of this experiment does not fall into one of the core, basic principles of persuasion but rather sits on the fringe to enhance them instead. This influence technique is known as the 'framing effect'. If advertisers are looking to reframe the cost of an expensive item, they use phrases such as "only pennies a day".

This technique is so powerful that since the phrase was used in a German newspaper advertisement in August 1960 to promote the Olympia typewriter, which was offered as "Yours... for just pennies a day." What makes the 'Pennies-a-day' sales technique so powerful is its ability to increase the saleability of products because few other methods can communicate a high degree of affordability to potential buyers so succinctly.

In the 1990s, Kellogg's ran popular adverts promoting their corn flakes telling shoppers that half a cup of milk and one serving of cornflakes costs less than 25 cents. This was reiterated by one shopper in their adverts, saying, "You can't even buy a postage stamp for 25 cents anymore". This form of advertising encourages consumers to make their own expense or price comparison without the company having to be as obvious and crude and detailing the price against other similar products.

EXPERIMENT 11

The question:

Imagine you are a University student and were approached by someone who introduced themselves as being from the County Youth Counselling Program. They make the following request:

"We're currently recruiting university students to work as voluntary, nonpaid counsellors at the County Juvenile Detention Centre. The position could require two hours of your time per week for a minimum of two years. You would be working more in the line of a big brother (or sister) to one of the boys (or girls) at the detention home. Would you be interested in being considered for one of these positions?"

YES / NO

If not, imagine you were approached by the same County Youth Counselling Programme Representative, and they asked the following:

"We're recruiting university students to chaperone a group of boys (girls) from County Juvenile Detention centre on a trip to the zoo. It would be voluntary, nonpaid, and would require about two hours of one afternoon or evening. Would you be interested in being considered for one of these positions?"

YES / NO

The experiment:

The experiment detailed above was the one carried out by prominent psychologist Robert Cialdini and his research team in 1975 to examine reciprocal concession procedures for inducing compliance.[21] This later became known as 'The Door-in-the-Face Technique'.

I'm sure your reply to offering two years of your life to the first scenario was 'no'. If so, you'd be no different to the 97% of the 58 students Cialdini, and his researchers asked, with just 3% agreeing to that commitment. The second question yielded a much greater sign-up, to the tune of 33% agreeing to volunteer for two hours an evening.

The experiment revealed its most surprising results when Cialdini and his team posed different combinations of questions. The 3 question variations were given different names: 'the rejection-moderation condition', 'the smaller request only control', and finally 'exposure control'.

Asking only the first question above did not form part of the final evaluation, because as expected, nearly everyone declined but was integral to the experiment.

The first part of the experiment applied the 'rejection-moderation condition'. Here the researchers posed the first question to the students, and when this was rejected, they immediately followed it up by asking the second question: "well, we also have another program you might be interested in". This resulted in a much more emphatic 50% of people signing up for the smaller request.

The second 'exposure control' researchers simply described the first condition and then the second one and then gave the participants a choice as to which one they wanted to participate in. This approach resulted in 25% of participants complying with the smaller request and 75% declining to take part in either.

Finally, when the 'smaller request on control' experiment was conducted, and the researchers asked the participants to sign up to the smaller request only, this yielded a 16.7% sign-up rate.

Principles of persuasion at work:

This experiment is loosely linked to the consistency principle of persuasion. The principle of consistency suggests that by committing to the act of doing something small such as filling out a petition or placing a poster in our window, increases the likelihood that we will commit to a much greater action further down the line, in keeping with the theme of the original smaller action we took. By declining to do something big (such as the voluntary 2-year commitment in the example above), we feel partly obliged to agree to a trade-off and compromise by committing to a smaller commitment.

The main persuasive technique in play here, however, is the 'foot-in-the-door' technique. Similar to the principle of consistency – once you have complied with a request for a small favour, you are more inclined to comply with a larger request in the future. If, however, you were asked for a larger request from the outset, without a smaller request being made first, this is called the 'door-in-the-face' technique. The theory behind this is that if we decline a request for something big, we feel bad and go along with an alternative request, which, in comparison, seems more trivial.

Not only is this technique effectively used in the sales and marketing industries, but without realizing it, we have nearly all been using these same techniques to influence and persuade others around us since we were young. As children, we may have asked our parents for some money to buy some sweets and then, once they agreed, asked for a bit more. Alternatively, we may have asked them to stay up a bit later to watch a program on TV and then asked them to watch one more show after their initial agreement.

EXPERIMENT 12

The question:

Do you believe that holding something heavy would subconsciously influence you to place more importance on a subject you were being asked about, compared to if you were holding something light?

YES / NO

The experiment:

Whilst this experiment may sound like it belongs on the fringes of genuine questions and investigations into behavioural psychology, in 2009, psychologists Jostmann, Lakens, and Schubert put this idea suggested in the question to the test.[22] In order to determine whether weight influenced people to give increased importance to a subject, the researchers stopped University students and asked them to answer some thought-provoking questions.

Questions included those focusing on their satisfaction with the mayor, their perceptions on the quality of city life, or, more specifically, "how important do you think it is that the student body has a voice in the college decision-making process?" The students were each stopped at random and were given one of two differently weighted clipboards to record the answers to these questions. The two clipboards weighed 2.29 pounds (or 1,039 grams) and 1.45

pounds (or 658 grams, respectively). Each student was asked to decide on the importance of each question using a sliding 1 to 7 scale and record their results.

The researcher's suspicions were confirmed when results recorded by students were averaged out. Those using the heavier clipboard expressed an average 5.27 satisfaction rating in response to the questions posed, whilst the students holding the lighter clipboards expressed an average 4.21 satisfaction rating. The researchers' evaluation of the results suggests that people place more importance on a particular issue of a subject if they are holding something heavy compared to if they are holding something light.

However, at the time and today, there is a significant amount of controversy surrounding this experiment as four other research teams have replicated this, with only one of them producing similar but not quite as conclusive results as the original experiment conducted by Jostmann and his team. There is a possibility that the results from Jostmann's experiment were a fluke, and as the subsequent three experiments do not support the original experiment, the controversy remains but is certainly food for thought and a welcome quirk in the field of influence and behavioural psychology.

Principles of persuasion at work:

Whilst there are no core principles of persuasion in play here, the results of Jostmanns' experiment support the widely held belief that your body can strongly influence your thinking. (Self-influence). This is also referred to as 'embodied cognition'.

Amy Cuddy, a Harvard psychologist, also shares some intriguing insights into the relationship between our body, our mind, and the influential effect it can have on us and those around us. In her popular TED talk, 'Your body language may shape who you are', she reiterates how people in positions of power often adopt a very open body posture - be it through their hands on their hips, hands behind their head, or legs wide apart. All these postures essentially take up more space. Behaving or acting with these dominant poses can convey authority to others – a powerful principle of persuasion.

These characteristics or behaviours can also be seen in the animal with animals such as pythons, swans, or baboons all opening up their bodies to exert their dominance or power. Based on these observations, Cuddy and her team conducted several experiments in which participants posed in 'power poses' such as hands-on their hips, feet spread apart and flat on the floor, or fist-pumped in the air. Following this, they then took part in a filmed, gruelling interview (as an interviewee) in which the interviewer purposefully didn't react to their answers. Independent evaluators then watched back the videos of the participants and were able to correctly identify those participants who came across as the most 'powerful' as those people who had primed themselves for the interview by adopting 'power poses'. Cuddy concluded that adopting a powerful pose or posture of dominance, such as hands placed on the hips and legs apart (like Wonder Woman) during part of the day, can, in fact, increase your confidence and encourage you to take more risks, with both traits associated with influential behaviour.

EXPERIMENT 13

The question:

Would you be more likely to agree to a negotiation deal if the seller agreed to throw in his pet frog to sweeten the deal (and the final offer was close, but not exactly what you were hoping for anyway)?

YES / NO

The experiment:

In 1981, psychologists Karen O'Quinn and Joel Aronoff wanted to investigate whether the injection of humour into a negotiation would put a prospective customer in a better mood and, as a result, make them more cooperative in a negotiation situation.[23]

In the experiment, undergraduate research participants were asked to negotiate the price of a piece of artwork with the seller. The undergraduates (or buyers) were made a final offer at the end of the negotiation in which half of the participants were offered $6,000 whilst the other half were offered $6,000 plus a little humour. In this case, the buyer would say, "Well, the final amount I'll accept is $6,000, and I'll throw in my pet frog". This injected humour proved highly influential with the participants, conceding much less on their final purchase price than the participants with who the seller had not shared some of his light-hearted comedy with.

The injection of comedy worked both on men and women in equal measure, and as predicted, O'Quinn and Aronoff found that humour-induced subjects made more concessions to the purchase price.

Principles of persuasion at work:

Here, likeability is the principle of persuasion, and in this case, it is gained through humour. As with all experiments associated with likeability, it is essential to behave authentically, otherwise, any tricks you may be employing to be seen as likeable will quickly become transparent. Placing just as much interest in their needs as yours and actively addressing those needs is the easiest route to becoming more likeable.

In a subsequent experiment in 1986 to support these findings, Peter Carnevale and Alice Isen studied negotiator abilities to reach collaborative agreements in negotiation.[24] They found that the agreements were met when the negotiation was more sociable and pleasant feelings were induced. This resulted in the needs of both parties being met when both parties used fewer contrived tactics and were happy to make more concessions. This meant that overall, they achieved higher joint outcomes.

EXPERIMENT 14

The question:

Does the carrot (reward) approach to persuading children to study hard at school actually work?

YES /NO

The experiment:

In 1973, Stanford psychologist Mark Lepper and his team set out to examine the truth behind the question posed above to determine if children's intrinsic interest increases with an extrinsic reward.[25]

Lepper and his researchers visited a school and told one group of students that they would be rewarded with 'good player' medals for their drawings whilst the other group of students was given no such promise. When Lepper and his team returned to the school a few days later and gave drawing tasks to the two sets of students, they found that those who had been promised the reward in the form of a medal spent a significantly shorter length of time on their drawings compared to the other group who had had no promises made to them.

Lepper and his team concluded that the reasoning behind this was because children associate rewards for doing things they don't like.

For example, "Eat all your vegetables, and you can have pudding".

Principles of persuasion at work:

To some extent, this contradicts reciprocity as a principle of persuasion here, perhaps as these principles apply differently to children. As adults, we are rewarded for doing something well and are motivated by the possibility of a reward. This could be a physical gift, pay rise, or promotion. With children, if you set them an activity that they enjoy, any rewards that you offer them may detract from their enjoyment of the task and, as a result, demotivate them. They have psychologically reframed what they once considered play into work. As a result, evidence shows that the techniques used to motivate children are different from those used to motivate adults. In schools, motivation shouldn't come from rewards but instead from an engaging curriculum and a caring atmosphere that nurtures their natural sense of curiosity.

It's worth noting, however, that occasionally, psychological principles can become skewed when working with children, as they have few, if any, responsibilities in their lives. Furthermore, the world and life itself is still evolving around them, and as a result, they only begin to understand the concept of influence and persuasion the older they get, making them just as susceptible as adults are. Take happiness, for example. When we are young, something had to happen to upset us because we were generally always happy. The older we get, the more this notion has reversed, and something has to make us happy. Based on all of this evidence, it is clear that children respond to very different persuasive messages than adults. As a result, due consideration should be given to the language and approach you take when trying to motivate, persuade or influence a child, compared to an adult.

EXPERIMENT 15

The question:

What do you think interviewers look for most when interviewing their applicants:

A. Their Qualifications B. Their Experience C. Their Personality

The experiment:

In 2004, psychologists Higgins and Trust conducted an experiment to determine the effect of applicant influence tactics and recruiter perceptions.[26] Most people think interviewers look at the qualifications and level of experience that an applicant has before making a decision, but there is another factor of influence at play too.

Higgins, Trust, and their team began by assessing 116 student applications for a job via a pre-interview survey they had completed at the university placement office. They specifically measured the two factors that interviewers regularly say are of utmost importance in interviews: work experience and qualifications.

After the interview that they attended, each of the applicants was then asked to complete a questionnaire to evaluate if they think they had communicated their strengths to the best of their ability to the interviewer. They were also quizzed to see if they had taken an interest in the company and asked the interviewer what type of applicant they were looking for and responded appropriately to both.

The team of researchers also probed the interviewers for their feedback too. They wanted to establish if these same interviewees had possessed the appropriate qualifications and experience for the role, how well they would integrate into the company, and the main question – if they would be offered the job or not.

After assimilating the data and plotting it all out, they discovered that the candidates chosen were those who had the most pleasant personalities. Smiling and eye contact was recognized as important. Equally so, it was those who had spent time discussing more than the job or anything that the interviewer and candidate had a mutual interest in.

Principles of persuasion at work:

Likeability is clearly the principle of persuasion at work here and could not be more emphatically demonstrated than in this experiment. The interviewers had chosen their applicants less on their qualifications and experience but more on their positive personality and likeability.

It is worth noting that likeability will not get you every position you apply for, and you would still need some elements of required qualifications and experience, but certainly, when it comes to a tie-breaker between several candidates with similar strengths, likeability will certainly be the winning ticket.

EXPERIMENT 16

The question:

Which of these two American companies do you think performed best on the stock market?

A. Barning's Inc. B. Aegeadux Inc

A / B

The experiment:

In 2006, psychologists Adam Alter and Daniel Oppenheimer from Princetown University invited 29 students to rate the fluency level of a random sample of genuine company names listed on the stock market.[27] Using their ratings, they then invested money in 20 of the companies which had the most easily and least easily pronounced names.

They found that over the first year's performance, $1,000 invested in the ten companies rated to have the most easily pronounced names netted $333 more profit than another $1,000 invested in 10 companies with less easily pronounced names.

In answer to the question posed at the start of this experiment, Oppenheimer and Alter found that the names such as Barning's Inc. (more easily pronounced) outperformed companies with names such as Aegeadux Inc. (less easily pronounced).

Further research showed that the association between a company's name and its share price was sometimes due to simpler company names conveying a more appealing meaning. A more easily pronounced ticker code (used for abbreviations on TV and websites) belonging to a company also outperformed those which were more challenging on the tongue. Names such as KAR outperformed RDO by an average daily increase in profit of $85.35. If you consider that in 2013 the average daily trading value was approximately US$169 billion, these differences have a massive impact on profits and losses.

Principles of persuasion at work:

There is no real principle of persuasion in play here, but it does hark back to the acronym K.I.S.S. short for Keep it Simple, Stupid. People are not solely influenced by larger companies having simpler names but are also more drawn towards names that are straightforward to pronounce and easy to remember.

EXPERIMENT 17

The question:

For those of you who remember The Weakest Link – a UK general knowledge-based game show where the participants can vote one another off, which members in the semi-circle are more likely to be voted off, regardless of their answers?

A. Players standing in the central positions
B. Players standing at the most extreme ends of the semi-circle

A / B

The experiment:

In 2006 Priya Raghubi and Ana Valenzuela conducted an experiment that analyzed episodes of the aforementioned Weakest Link game show to determine whether the other competitors are more influenced to vote you out of the game dependent on the position that you stand.[28]

They found that, on average, those players standing in the central position of the semi-circle reached the final round 42% of the time and won the game 45% of the time whilst those on the fringes, and in particular the most extreme wings of the semi-circle reached the final round just 17% of the time and reached the final a mere 10% of the time.

In another experiment conducted by the same psychologists, participants were shown five photographs of a mixture of men and women with no distinguishing features and asked which ones they would choose for a particular internship. Candidates in the centre of the group were chosen significantly more often than those on the edges.

Principles of persuasion at work:

Whilst there are no official principles of persuasion relevant in this example, the results of the second experiment do support the first. People are more influenced to choose people or participants who are in the centre of a group rather than at the edges. Psychologists label this effect the 'centre-stage effect,' and this should be considered if you are taking part in an assessment-based exercise where you want to influence the assessors into choosing you.

EXPERIMENT 18

The question:

If you are attending an interview as an applicant, and your past history included the fact that you had not completed a school semester because you had been expelled for cheating, is it better to share this information at the start or the end of the interview?

START / END

The experiment:

In 1972, psychologists Edward Jones and Eric Gordon from Duke University wanted to determine whether it is better to place potentially negative information at the beginning or end of an interview.[29] To help answer this, they considered the question posed above.

The two researchers invited several participants to watch a video about a man who was faced with the aforementioned dilemma. He was, of course, stooged for this experiment, and as a result, the researchers were able to edit the tape so that two interview sequences were produced.

Jones, Gordon, and their team played the first interview where the man revealed his expulsion and cheating at the start of his interview to one group of participants. The man revealed his misdemeanours at the end of his interview in a second interview to another set of participants. Each group of participants was then interviewed to determine how likeable they found the man.

The researchers found that when the misdemeanours were mentioned at the start of the interview, the man was perceived to be much more likeable than when his issues were mentioned at the end.

The researchers also made further use of their participants by inviting them to watch another video, but this time, rather than hear about a negative experience being disclosed, such as cheating and expulsion, a piece of good fortune was shared. The response from the participants was now reversed, and the man was more likeable when the good fortune was disclosed towards the end of the interview.

Other conclusions were drawn from their investigations too. They found that the most appropriate point in the interview to disclose the piece of bad fortune was also dependent on whose responsibility it was. In this instance, the responsible person who disclosed their bad fortune early on was deemed more likeable than the late discloser. However, when the person was not responsible for a piece of bad fortune, he was liked more if the event was disclosed later on in the interview.

Principles of persuasion at work:

Likeability is the principle of persuasion at work here. In the first few chapters of this book, I outlined that people are more inclined to say 'yes' to people they like. Find a similarity, offer a compliment, and maybe demonstrate that you have shared goals are three tips to increasing your likeability in an interview.

In terms of the timing around self-disclosure of personal information and its direct relationship with influence, lawyers are judged to have a stronger case when they present a weakness in their argument at the start of a trial. Presenting your openness at the start of an interview demonstrates your vulnerability and authenticity early on. It also communicates your integrity and strength of character to share your struggles first as opposed to mislead the jury with your positive personality traits first. When considering placing your positive traits in your responses, consider placing them at the end, and remember to remain modest when describing an experience or event.

EXPERIMENT 19

The question:

Imagine, if you will, that I am a researcher, and I invite you along to my behavioural psychology laboratory to participate in a study. I then arrange for you to win some money. Once you leave the lab, one of my research team interviews you about the study and then inform you that I had used my own money to fund the research, and I'm now running low on money. My research assistant then asks if you would mind returning the money. This is scenario A.

Scenario B starts the same as scenario A with you having won the money, but this time, as you leave the lab, you are approached by a researcher who tells you a different story. This time, he informs you that the psychology department had financed the experiment, and it's them who are running low on money, and would you mind returning your winnings? This is scenario B.

Do you feel greater empathy (and preference) to the researcher in scenario A or B?

A / B

The experiment:

The experiment played out much the same as you have read above.[30]

The researchers polled the participants' answers as to which of the two researchers (that asked for the money back) they preferred. They found that overall, the participants who had helped the researcher in scenario A and who cited more personal reasons to request the return of the money were preferred over the researcher in Scenario B who's reasons for returning the money were on behalf of the department.

Principles of persuasion at work:

The results of this simple experiment can be associated with the reciprocity and likeability principles of persuasion. Russian novelist Leo Tolstoy eloquently stated that:

"We do not love people so much for the good they have done us, as for the good we do them".

This particular phenomenon is more commonly known as the Franklin effect due to a story recorded from the 18th century. In it, American politician Benjamin Franklin wanted to win over the support of an apathetic member of the Pennsylvania state council. Rather than attempting to curry favour by showering him in compliments, Franklin asked him if he could borrow a rare book from his book collection. He agreed, and Franklin is quoted to say that from that point on, he was in "readiness to serve me on all occasions". More simply put, in order to influence someone to like you, encourage them to do you a favour. It should be noted that the Franklin effect is more likely to work on someone using small favours as a request, whereas larger favours may be reluctantly agreed or, even worse, refused. In both the original example and the example above, they equally emphasize that people are more influenced by the human, personal approach.[31]

EXPERIMENT 20

The question:

Imagine you listen to two tape recordings. Both relate to a student taking part in a quiz, detailing their participation, and then sharing some information about their background.

In both tape recordings, the student scores an admirable 90% on the quiz. In the first tape recording (A), he describes a lifetime of success. In the second recording (B), however, at the end of the tape recording, he is heard accidentally spill a cup of coffee over his new suit and ruin it.

Do you find the participant in student A or B more likeable?

A / B

The experiment:

In 1966, psychologists Elliot Aronson, Ben Willerman, and Joanne Floyd wanted to study the effects that embarrassing failures or mistakes may have on increasing or decreasing our level of attractiveness.[32] They conducted the experiment with participants listening to the above recordings and then being asked to rate how likeable they found the student they heard. Both recordings were staged with the student faking the knocking over of the coffee cup.

The same student was used in both recordings, and the participants could not see them and only hear them, thus would not be swayed by visual stimuli.

Despite the only difference between the two recordings being the fictitious knocking over of the coffee cup, all the students considered the student who had spilt their coffee in recording B much more likeable.

Principles of persuasion at work:

Again we look at the likeability principle of persuasion. In this instance, a moment of vulnerability and imperfection makes the student seem more authentic and relatable. This particular principle is also known as the 'pratfall effect. Whilst it could be argued that the results may differ if there is a visual element too, British psychologist, Dr Richard Wiseman from the University of Hertfordshire put this to the test in his TV show, called '*The People Watchers*'. In it, he conducted an experiment in which he asked two demonstrators (stooges) to deliver a presentation to sell a blender.

The first demonstrator, Sara, spent all night learning her lines and perfecting her pitch and, as a result, gave a perfect visual demonstration to an audience the following day. The smoothie was perfectly made and presented, and her demonstration was met with appreciative applause.

Emma, the second demonstrator, also a stooge, demonstrated her pitch, but this time the lid flew off, and she was covered in part-pulped smoothie juice. This demonstration was met with a more sympathetic round of applause. At the end of the experiment, the audience members were asked three questions:

1. Which of the participants impressed you the most?
2. Which of the two would you be most likely to buy from?
3. Which of the participants did you like the most?

Overall, Sara was seen as the more professional and Emma the more likeable, reiterating the strength of the pratfall effect and the warmth people feel to others who are more relatable, much like our Guinness World Record Holder car salesman mentioned earlier.

EXPERIMENT 21

The question:

Imagine you are one of the delegates at one of my influence keynotes. As a thank you for attending and participating, I give you a beautiful mug as a gift. A bit later on in the seminar, you are chatting with your colleagues, and you find out that not only did some of the other delegates also received a mug but others, who didn't get one was given a luxury chocolate bar instead. Both gifts cost me exactly the same. You love chocolate. Do you keep your mug, or do you ask to swap it?

KEEP IT / SWAP IT

The experiment:

Before we get to the answer, I want to share some other experiments with you to give you some background before discussing more about the question I posed to you.

Has anyone ever given you something, and then they ask for it back? Have you ever borrowed something from someone else, and then you decided you wanted one of your own? The principle behind these thought processes is called the 'endowment principle'.

In 1991, psychologists Daniel Kahneman, Jack Knetsch, and Richard

Thaler conducted a study to explore the endowment principle in greater detail to understand how it can influence our decision-making abilities.[33] For this experiment, they recruited a number of participants and assigned them different roles, either buyers or sellers.

The sellers were all given free mugs as gifts. After some time had elapsed for them to become attached to their mugs, Kahneman and his team then asked the sellers how much they were prepared to sell their mugs to the buyers. They then asked a group of participants who didn't receive a gift and didn't even know they had been given as gifts how much they were prepared to buy the mugs off the sellers for. Despite the mugs being given as gifts, the sellers placed an average value on their mugs of $7.12, whilst the buyers were prepared to pay an average of $2.87 per mug.

The reason behind this is based on the 'endowment principle'. The endowment effect is an emotional bias towards something that you own. Once we take ownership of something (in this case, the mug), we irrationally over-value it regardless of its objective value. People appreciate the things they physically own a lot more than if they didn't, and as a result, their fear of losing them is higher. This is known as loss aversion. Emotionally loss aversion causes us to feel a pain that is twice as strong as pleasure at an equal gain.

In 2000, psychologists Ziv Carmon and Dan Ariely wanted to see if the same results would occur outside of a behavioural psychology laboratory in the real world.[34] At Duke University, their basketball games are always oversubscribed, so to give everyone an equal chance to attend, the University runs a lottery a few days before, where the seats at the chosen games can be won as prizes. Carmon and Ariely tracked down the winners and asked them how much they would be prepared to sell their tickets for. The winners said that they were willing to sell their tickets for an average of $2,400, giving the reason that the game was an important one and they didn't want to miss it. This demonstrated the principle of loss aversion.

The lottery losers, however, offered a much lower price to buy the tickets, 14 times less in fact, to the tune of $175. Conversely to those who had randomly won the tickets, those who hadn't valued the tickets much less as they didn't have any ownership over them. When interviewed further, the people who didn't win in the lottery spoke more about the value of money they didn't spend and still had rather than the tickets they could have won.

By now, the pieces should be in place for me to review the question I posed earlier. In one of the networking events I hosted, I conducted this simple experiment with the guests attending. I randomly gave out a mug and a chocolate bar to the attendees. At the end of the event, I then told the delegates that they were more than welcome to keep their free gift or exchange it with someone else. Statistically, 50% of the people would keep their item whilst 50% would change. However, just 10% of the attendees decided to swap their items, reiterating the power of the endowment principle. People fall in love with what they already have or have just been given; in this example, it was a mug or a chocolate bar. It just shows that people are prepared to pay more to retain something they already have or have just been given.

Principles of persuasion at work:

When we take ownership over something, we start to evaluate things from that perspective as the loss aversion principle kicks in. Knowing that losses are more important in our decision-making processes, we can leverage this in prospective clients when it comes to influencing the outcome of a negotiation. The endowment principle is applied in many different businesses and, with a little creativity, can be applied to influence prospective customers to buy your products and services too.[35]

The endowment principle works extremely well alongside the reciprocity principle of persuasion. One example of these two principles working in unison includes offering your customers free pricing or free trials on your product or service. This is a small gift in itself, which activates the principle of reciprocity.

Another example would be to offer your customers the option to use one of your basic packages or something with limited features (free pricing). If they then feel that this product or service meets their needs, then they would have already felt a degree of ownership to the product or service, and the endowment effect starts to influence their desire to access more advanced features.

The same is true for products and services that are initially offered for a free trial. When the free trial period ends, the prospective buyer's aversion to loss makes it difficult for them to turn back now they have psychologically placed ownership on it.

This principle is also what makes money-back guarantees or the offer of a refund if someone isn't 100% satisfied so successful too. Rarely do people pursue these refunds or cancellations of subscriptions as they have taken ownership. However, it is important to note that the endowment effect only works here if the client sees value in what they have. If you are giving a free trial for something which doesn't work and only marginally meets their needs, then they will be able to distance themselves from the ownership of it and be happy to ask for the refund or leave the trial period without taking psychological ownership of it.

Allowing people to be physically hands-on with a product or service is by far the strongest way for a potential client to feel a connection with an item and place ownership on it. By allowing people to try on a comparatively expensive jacket in a shop or handle the latest iPhone as examples, they eventually create a future projection of themselves wearing it or using it respectively. This then influences their price perspective.

This is one of the main reasons that Apple showrooms place such importance on the display of their products and encourage people to try them in-store. This method is so successful it generates Apple sales of nearly $6,000 per square foot per year.

Whilst you may think this powerful principle is only applicable to smaller items like jackets or phones, it's equally applicable to larger items too. Encouraging prospective clients to test drive the cars they are interested in results in a far higher number of sales than if they were just to be told about its specifications. By sitting themselves behind the wheel, again, they are able to pretend they are the owner and create a mental projection of themselves owning it in the future, making them more likely to purchase it.

EXPERIMENT 22

The question:

In chapter 11, we examined how The 'Door-in-the-Face' technique could be used to convince the target to comply with a large request, for which they are likely to decline, and then ask a smaller request (which is hopefully agreed upon, and is in fact, the actual result you wanted at the start).

Within the world of influence and psychology, there is also the 'Foot-in-the-Mouth' technique. This particular strategy involves asking for a relatively straightforward task to be completed, and then, regardless of what the other person says, you ask immediately for a second, increasingly difficult task to be done.

Based on these two styles of influence, do you think that the Foot-in-the-Mouth or Door-in-the-Face technique or a combination would produce the best results when attempting to influence someone?

Foot-in-the-Mouth technique / Door-in-the-Face technique / Combination of both

The experiment:

The purpose of this experiment, conducted by Valerie Fointiat in 2000, was to compare the effectiveness of the Foot-in-the-Mouth and

Door-in-the-Face techniques.[36] For this experiment, Fointiat and her team of researchers visited 90 French homemakers posing as members of a charitable association, collecting food for the needy people of the town. Their goal was to obtain a donation.

Thirty of the homemakers were asked for a donation using the 'foot-in-the-mouth' technique. Another thirty were asked for a donation using a combination of Foot-in-the-Mouth and Door-in-the-Face techniques, whilst the final third remained as the control group, and a direct request was made with the omission of either of the techniques above.

The large request was to donate food every week for three months, and the smaller request was simply for a single, smaller donation.

8 out of 30 people in the control group agreed to the target request, 12 out of 30 in the foot-in-mouth request group agreed to the request, whilst 18 out of 30 people in the Foot-in-the-Mouth-Door-in-the-Face group agreed to the request for a donation. This shows that a combination of both Foot-in-the-Mouth and Door-in-the-Face techniques was most effective when persuading people to donate food for charity.

Principles of persuasion at work:

Whilst there are no direct principles of persuasion at work here, it is apparent that a combination of Foot-in-the-Mouth and Door-in-the-Face techniques is the most effective if you want to influence somebody into doing something. (In this example, donating food to charity)

If you were to apply these principles in your work, social or personal life, you could begin by increasing the compliance for the desired target request by making a simpler and easier first request. (The foot-in-the-door procedure) This could then be followed up with the door-in-the-face technique in which you can increase compliance even further by making an extremely difficult request and then following this up with a target request. (The one that is the desired outcome) By making two initial requests to precede the target request yields the greatest result and is the most powerful influence and persuasion strategy.

EXPERIMENT 23

The question:

Please rate the following sentences on a scale of 1-10 as to how accurately they describe human behaviour:

1. Life is mostly strife.
2. Life is mostly a struggle.
3. What sobriety conceals, alcohol reveals.
4. What sobriety conceals, alcohol unmasks.
5. Caution and measure will win you the treasure.
6. Caution and measure will win you riches.

The experiment:

In 2000, Matthew McGlone and Jessica Tofighbakhsh and her team invited several participants to read the sentences above and give each a rating to see how accurately it describes the world.[37] They found that although the participants did not believe that rhyming was in any way indicative of accuracy levels, they all agreed that the rhyming statements were perceived as significantly more accurate than those that didn't.

Principles of persuasion at work:

This experiment clearly focuses on the power of likeability. Psychologists McGlone and Tofighbakhsh both agreed that the rhyming statements were perceived as more accurate than those that didn't because it makes them more memorable, likeable, and repeatable. Current rhyming slogans such as 'A Mars a day helps you work rest and play', 'Beanz Meanz Heinz' and 'Gillette, the best a man can get are easily remembered and recalled.

EXPERIMENT 24

The question:

Read the following couple sentences with your third finger up to the sky and the others closed in a fist.

"Donald spent the next day at home. Around midday, his landlord came round asking him for his rent. Donald point blank refused, arguing that he would pay, but only after the landlord would complete the repairs to his flat, he had promised. They were at loggerheads."

What do you think of Donald? Are you in agreement with his behaviour of not paying?

YES / NO.

Now give this passage to someone else to read, but before they do, ask them to make a fist and raise their thumb and ask them what they thought of Donal and if *they* were more or less in agreement with Donald's behaviour than you?

The experiment:

In 2008, psychologists Jesse Chandler and Norbert Schwarz decided to investigate how extending your middle finger (swearing) affects your perception of others.[38]

They conducted an experiment similar to the one above using a similar paragraph describing Donald's day and gathered fifty-eight right-handed undergraduates to participate. The passage about Donald was read out twice, the first time with the participants raising their middle finger (as though they were swearing) and the second time extended their thumb up (as in positive recognition of something). The researchers avoided using the words 'middle finger,' which is often synonymous with swearing ('giving someone the middle finger') to avoid the participants making the association that this is what this experiment was evaluating, and thus distorting their answers.

After both passages had been read and the corresponding hand gestures made, the participants were asked their views on Donald. Those who had raised their middle finger whilst the passage was being read out perceived him as aggressive, whilst those who were asked to raise their thumbs thought he was less aggressive and more likeable.

Another study also evaluated the subconscious effect our physical actions have on our emotions and perceptions.[39] This time, a number of students were invited to attend a presentation (conducted by a team of researchers) where they were informed that their tuition fees might be going up. Some of the students were asked to nod their heads up and down, whilst others were asked to shake their heads from side to side. Again, so as not to alert the participants to the underlying premise of the experiment, they were told to move their head up and down rather than 'nod' it and to move their head from side to side rather than 'shake' it. At the end of the presentation, the students were asked how much they felt their tuition fees should increase by. Those who had been nodding their head suggested that their tuition fees should rise by a much higher amount than those who had been shaking their heads.

Principles of persuasion at work:

Whilst these two experiments are not linked to any principles of persuasion per se, they do have a relationship with self-influence and self-consensus. The way you act on the outside can have a direct effect on your emotions and behaviours on the inside. These same correlations can be drawn with gossiping too. Studies have shown that whatever traits you assign to another person through gossiping, people will just as likely associate them with you too, and as a result, their traits will be perceived as part of your personality.[40]

From an evolutionary perspective, one reason suggested as to why we nod our heads up and down in affirmation and side to side in denial is that infants often move their heads up and down when searching for the mother's breast and move their head side by side when they have finished feeding. If you want to increase your persuasive abilities to encourage others to agree with you, nod your head subtly to trigger a reciprocated response of affirmation and positivity.

EXPERIMENT 25

The question:

Would you buy an 'Internet Delivered Television' if this was being promoted by Arnold Schwarzenegger?

YES / NO

If your answer is yes, then you have simply been influenced by an authority figure – in this case - Arnold Schwarzenegger. I'm sure you'd agree that despite Arnold being an expert in weight lifting and blowing things up, he is by no means an expert in the field of internet-delivered television, and his authority in the film or weight lifting fields shouldn't be relevant here. However, despite this, you were subconsciously influenced by his overall authority status in different fields irrespective of whether he gave an expert opinion on the comparative merits of the product.

With that in mind, a few days later, you see another advert for a product called Excedrin (an over-the-counter pain relief headache and migraine reliever) presented by Daniel Schroeder, Director at Minnesota Pain Institute. He claims that the medicine had "Five years of clinical trials, and testing revealed no adverse effects" and was "Twice the strength of normal aspirin." Would you buy this medicine?

YES /NO

The experiment:

In 2002 Sagarin, Cialdini, and their team of researchers conducted an experiment called 'Dispelling the illusion of invulnerability: The motivations and mechanisms of resistance to persuasion.[41] The researchers wanted to test the notion that if you tell people about the persuasion tactics used in adverts and how they influence us, would it lessen their power of influence over us. They conducted an experiment similar to the one detailed above in which they showed 320 undergraduate students, first an advert with Arnold Schwarzenegger (not an authority in the field which he was promoting), then with Daniel Schroeder (a genuine or authority in his field). The same as I have attempted to simulate above, after watching the first ad, the students were told about how we become vulnerable to influence when we are presented with someone of notoriety or commercial recognition advertising the product or service that they have no authority to be promoting.

The first ad involving Schwarzenegger proved extremely persuasive. However, after the students who had seen the first ad and were then informed of the principle of persuasion in use, they became much more sceptical about an ad with a genuine figure of authority in it. They had, in many ways, been inoculated by the idea of authority as a principle of persuasion and become much more sceptical than those who hadn't seen the ad with Schwarzenegger in it.

Principles of persuasion at work:

Here, of course, we see the 'authority' principle of persuasion as the dominant force of influence. Authority is used as a persuasive tool in all forms of advertising, marketing and influence, and has even leeched onto social media. Instagrammers, for example, who have no authority on a particular service or product are being paid to promote certain items through their online channels as 'brand ambassadors.

By being aware of the principles of persuasion at work, it's possible to inoculate yourself against these tactics. Inoculate is a pertinent word here, as you can see this same concept in play in the medical world. Most injections to prevent us from getting the flu, rabies, chickenpox, etc., contain a small amount of the particular virus in it. This allows our bodies to build up a resistance to it. In much the same way as being exposed to and acknowledging the persuasive techniques used online and face to face-to by companies to sell us products and services, this allowed us to form a resistance against it. For people who want to influence others, it gives them the opportunity to come up with more creative or inventive solutions to communicate these principles of persuasion to you without you realizing it, making it the exciting form of psychology and behavioural science that it is.

EXPERIMENT 26

The question:

If you witness a student having an epileptic fit, on a scale of 1-10, how sure are you that you would provide assistance in the following situations?

A. There was no one else around except you and the student.
B. There were five people who had gone over to help.
C. The student was surrounded by more than five people. (Many)

A / B / C

The experiment:

Whilst the following account is not so much an experiment as an account of a horrific incident, it can still be used to draw many inferences about persuasion and influence. On March 13, 1964, Kitty Genovese, a 28-year-old woman, was murdered. At 2.30 in the morning, she was stabbed, and her assailant (later identified as Winston Mosley) ran away, leaving Kitty's screams echoing in the street. Despite the fact that several of her neighbours, with whom she had lived next door to for several years, had seen the attack, they had all looked away, and only Robert Mozer recognized her scream as a plea for help. He did no more than to tell Kitty's attacker to "leave that girl alone". Mosley later returned to the scene of the crime on the same night and then stabbed Genovese again, raped her, robbed her then ran away.

The entire series of attacks took place over half an hour, but the police didn't receive a call until nearly an hour after the attack. Several witnesses claimed that they had called the police prior to that, but their calls were not treated with any priority. Others also claimed to have called but not reported to the operator the severity of the crime. Meanwhile, others thought of calling the police but assumed that some of her other neighbours would do it instead.

Two weeks after the attack, The New York Times published an article with a headline which read "37 Who Saw Murder Didn't Call the Police," and was supported with a quote from an unidentified neighbour that claimed he didn't call the police because he "didn't want to get involved."

Genovese's murder sent shockwaves around New York City. Many asked questions and gossiped, posing the question of how 37 people could hear and even see such a brutal attack taking place but do nothing to act? Social and behavioural psychologists began to explore the effects of groupthink (faulty decision making that can occur in groups as a result of forces that bring a group together) the diffusion of responsibility (whereby a person is less likely to take responsibility for action or inaction when others are present) and Kitty's case gave rise to a psychological concept called "the bystander effect".

It was the above story and rise of these psychological concepts that psychologists Bibb Latane and John Darley decided to explore in greater detail in a study conducted in 1968. Using the story of Kitty's murder as inspiration for their experiment, the researchers asked a student to fake an epileptic fit, and then they observed the length of time it would take for someone to provide assistance. They were particularly interested in whether more or fewer witnesses would have an effect on the likelihood of anyone in that group helping.

They repeated this experiment with different numbers of people witnessing the fit and found that the more witnesses there are, the chances of help being given dramatically goes down. In statistical terms, when there was only one other person around when the student had an epileptic fit, the chance of someone providing immediate assistance was 85%. However, when the number of people in the vicinity increased to 5, the chances of someone helping fell to just 30%.

Principles of persuasion at work:

Consensus is the principle of persuasion at work here. What one person does, or in this case doesn't do, others will follow suit. In the case of inaction, this has been labelled as 'the bystander effect.'

The death of Kitty Genovese and the lack of assistance provided by her friends and neighbours was so shocking that this has spawned a huge volume of research and experiments into the area exploring the bystander effect.

One of these other experiments was again conducted by Bibb Latane and his team.[42] In this experiment, they observed visitors to a doctor's waiting room. They wanted to see how many of the participants who, upon observing smoke seeping out from underneath the waiting room door, would report its occurrence. The results were equally profound as their previous experiment. When the participant was on their own, they reported the leak 75% of the time. However, when there were three other people in the waiting room, the smoke was reported only 38% of the time.

The bystander effect and diffusion of responsibility refer to the fact that as the number of bystanders increases - the personal responsibility that an individual bystander feels decreases.

This knowledge can be applied in business and marketing too. Rather than sending out blanket emails to people in your team or prospective clients or customers, send a message to each person individually to increase the chance that they will respond or react to your request.

EXPERIMENT 27

The question:

Question 1.

Would you be more inclined to do something if somebody surprised you with a drink?

YES / NO

Question 2.

Do you think that if you received a Christmas card from a stranger, you would be persuaded to send one back in return?

YES / NO

The experiments:

I'll start by spoiling the principle of persuasion in play here. The questions above associated with the experiments below focus on the powerful principle of reciprocity. In 1971, Dennis Regan, a lecturer at Cornell University, and his team conducted an experiment to examine the effects doing a favour and liking had on compliance.[43]

In this first experiment, related to question one above, Regan invited a number of participants to an art appreciation evening. They arrived and were met by a guide. In this instance, the guide was one of Regan's research team who was present to help facilitate the experiment under the guise of playing a guide. The guide (stooge) showed the participants around the art exhibition individually, asking them to rate the art they saw. Halfway through, the guide excused himself and went to get himself a drink from the free drinks table. After quenching his thirst, he returned with a bottle (albeit a free one) for the participant. Throughout the course of the experiment, the guide brought half the participants a drink back, and the other half of the participants, he returned empty-handed to act as the control group.

After he returned with either a drink or empty-handed and the participants had enjoyed this supposed generosity or not, he asked them if they would buy some raffle tickets off him at 25 cents each. He explained that he only had a few left to sell and that if he sold them all, he would be rewarded with a $50 prize. Regan and his research team found that those who were given a free drink bought twice as many raffle tickets as those who weren't given a drink.

Five years later, in 1976, psychologists Phillip Kunz and Micheal Woolcott conducted an experiment to explore this relationship between psychology and the principle of reciprocation even further using Christmas cards.[44] Over a period of two weeks, Kunz and Woolcott chose random people out of the phone directory and sent them each a Christmas card with a return address detailed inside. They wanted to see if people who received a Christmas card from a stranger would reciprocate by sending one back in return. As they initially thought, the majority of those random people they sent a Christmas card to sent one back.

Principles of persuasion at work:

Reciprocity, as I mentioned at the start, is, of course, the principle of persuasion here. The rule of reciprocation is a social norm where if somebody does something positive to or for you, you feel obliged to repay that favour. Marketers use a broad range of variations of this technique to influence potential customers to purchase their goods or services.

You can see the principle of reciprocation at work when a salesperson gives a freebie to a customer in the hope that they will be influenced to make a full purchase. Similarly, in the business arena, a leader may deliberately give his staff attention and mentorship and positions of responsibility or promotions in exchange for loyalty. Another method to activate reciprocity in others is by offering customers beneficial (often free) information, advice, tips, or hacks in exchange for signing up for future marketing offers and information about new product launches and events.

The principle of reciprocity covers two points. We help people we like, and we like people who help us. You will no doubt see that this principle straddles the likeability principle of persuasion and, when combined with reciprocity, forms a highly effective form of influence.

EXPERIMENT 28

The question:

This is a two-fold question. Imagine you found a wallet in the street. Which of the following three wallets would you be more likely to return to its rightful owner?

A. A wallet with a card suggesting that the owner had recently made a charitable donation.
B. A wallet with a photograph in it of either a baby, puppy, or family.
C. A wallet that contained none of the above. Do you treat them all equally?

A / B / C

The second part of this question is as follows. Let's say the wallet you found had a photograph inside it. Which of the wallets containing the following photographs would you be more likely to return to its' rightful owner?

A. A wallet containing a photograph of a smiling baby.
B. A wallet containing a photograph of a cute puppy.
C. A wallet containing a photograph of a happy family.
D. A wallet containing a photograph of a contented elderly couple.

A / B / C / D

The experiment:

In the 1960s and '70s, one of the most well-known psychological experiments at the time was to investigate what motivated people to return a lost wallet to its rightful owner. Harvey Hornstein and his team gained the most notoriety for their experiments, with one taking place in Manhattan.[45] In this experiment, they examined whether people would be more likely to return a lost wallet to its owner if it elicited a negative or positive emotion. For this experiment, Hornstein and his team of researchers collected data from 105 random pedestrians in Manhattan.

In it, they simulated the idea that the wallet had already been lost once before by placing an envelope on the street with the wallet poking out of the top. Around the wallet, they had wrapped a letter addressed to the wallet's owner. This implied that the wallet had been found once already and that whoever found it had put the wallet in the envelope and was about to post it back to the rightful owner but then lost it again. Any of the pedestrians who came across the envelope and wallet package then had a choice as to whether to post the envelope and wallet back to the original owner or not.

Hornstein, however, had simulated this experiment using two different notes wrapped around the wallets. The first 50 people, who found the wallet, read a note which elicited feelings of positivity. This particular note starting with "It's been a pleasure to help someone" and finished with "and really has been no problem at all".

The second note, however, elicited a much more negative emotion stating, "......having to return it has been a great inconvenience. I was quite annoyed at having to bother with the whole problem of returning it. I hope you appreciate the efforts that I have gone through".

The difference in wording between the two notes resulted in 40% of the unsuspecting participants returning the wallet back to its rightful owner when the note had more positivity in its tone. The wallet, which had a note with a more negative tone around it, was returned only 12% of the time.

British psychologist Dr Richard Wiseman from the University of Hertfordshire conducted a similar experiment to the one above.

Wiseman upped the ante here and bought 240 wallets. He then separated them out into batches of 48. In each one of the batches, he added a photograph of a smiling baby, cute puppy, happy family, and elderly couple, respectively. The final batch, he filled with everyday items such as receipts, membership cards, raffle tickets, and discount vouchers but no additional photographs to act as the control group. All of these were then secretly dropped in high footfall areas on the streets of Edinburgh.

Over the course of the following year, 88% of the wallets that contained a photograph of a smiling baby had been returned. The photograph of a cute puppy secured a return rate of 53%, photo of a happy family 48% return rate, elderly couple 28% return rate, whilst the control wallet, with no emotion eliciting photo inside, only 15% were returned. In summary, 9/10 people returned the wallet containing a baby picture, whereas 1/7 people returned the control wallet containing no picture.

Principles of persuasion at work:

Whilst there are no direct principles of persuasion at work here, the fact that the wallets containing positive notes or a smiling baby to influence people to return the respective wallets could certainly be linked to likeability. People are more likely to do things for people that they like. This is certainly the case in relation to the first experiment conducted by Hornstein. In the case of Wiseman's experiment, it could be argued that the deep-seated evolutionary mechanism kicks in and is related to our protective gene, and that encourages us to return the wallet with the photograph of the baby in it.

There are countless studies and experiments that have been conducted to understand why a baby's face can be so persuasive, but those are perhaps beyond the scope of this book. That said, a baby's face does reflect innocence, kindness, lack of aggression, sensitivity, and other appealing personality traits. These are all traits we should aim to nurture within ourselves to deliver authentic levels of likeability, one of the most powerful principles of persuasion.

EXPERIMENT 29

The question:

Would you allow a group of men to come over to your house and audit your household items for a public service publication?

YES / NO

The experiment:

By mid-way through 1966, Jonathan Freedman and Scott Fraser had made a name for themselves for investigating the foot-in-the-door technique.[46] This is the idea you could influence someone to undertake a large action or request by first undertaking a much smaller one. In this next experiment, Freedman, Fraser, and their research team called a number of people to ask permission if their team of 5 or 6 men could come round their house, scour their cupboards and conduct a full audit on all of their household items. The team grounded their request by stating that they were making this rather bold request as they were writing a feature article in the public service publication "The Guild". Unsurprisingly a large number refused, but surprisingly 22% agreed to take part in this rather invasive house search, usually reserved for raids by an intelligence agency or police.

For the second experiment, the team called a different group of homeowners and made a much more straightforward and digestible request: would they be happy to answer a few questions about which household items they use so that the information given could be used in a publication called 'The Guild'. The majority of homeowners agreed.

Three days later, the researchers called this second group again, making the same request as in the first experiment - asking if they would be happy with several men coming round to audit their household items just to ensure it tallied with the answers that they'd given. This time a much larger percentage of people agreed to this bigger request, to the tune of 53% in agreement.

Principles of persuasion at work:

Again we see consensus, commitment, and consistency as the principles of persuasion at work with the foot-in-the-door technique supercharging these principles. Whilst it has been mentioned before about how these techniques can be applied in business and at work, they are equally applicable and effective at home and in one's personal life.

These techniques can be applied to changing to a more active and healthy lifestyle. Taking a couch to 5k challenge doesn't start with the 5k run but with signing up to a gym or an online training program. Even then, the small step may be as simple as walking around the block or running on the spot for 10 minutes. As with many things related to self-improvement, starting with a small action quickly builds momentum. For example, running on the spot for 15 minutes may end up being 30 minutes because you've put your gym clothes on, you're hot and sweaty anyway, and you're not doing anything else.

As a result, this one small initial step can influence you to take a much larger step and degree of commitment.

EXPERIMENT 30

The question:

Would you say you are ethical and moral?

YES / NO

If so, do you act morally and ethically and in line with your beliefs, or do you prefer to appear moral and ethical because the associated costs and trade-offs are too high?

For example, you say you care about the environment, but you will still eat foods that contain palm oil even though you may know that rainforests would have to be cut down in order to create palm tree plantations. As a result, the planting and growing of palm trees is one of the leading contributors to the deforestation of rainforests

YES / NO

The experiment:

In 2002, psychologist Daniel Batson from Kansas University set out to expand upon Bickamn's work to determine whether people genuinely act in an ethical and moral way or simply like the idea of appearing to be ethical and moral because of the associated costs are too high for them.[47] For example, they want to care about the environment but would prefer to drive a fancy car than take public transport. This is also known as 'moral hypocrisy'.[48]

Batson and his team asked several participants a number of questions and to rate how moral and ethical they believe they are. Questions included whether they believe they do the right thing, believe in a just world, or are concerned about the wellbeing of others.

Batson invited these participants to his lab and informed them that there was another participant in an adjacent room. He gave the first participant a coin and told them if they flip it, and it landed on heads, they would win a raffle ticket, and if it landed on tails, they would have to spend 30 minutes adding up a series of numbers (a mundane task). Batson also told the participant that he or his team would not be checking the outcome of the coin toss and would leave it to their honesty.

Whilst the throw of a coin would statistically come up heads and tails 50% of the time, respectively, 90% of the participants said that the coin had landed heads up, thus qualifying them for the raffle ticket. Moreover, and just as importantly, by announcing that the coin had landed heads up, it excludes them from the mundane task – or more to the point, assigning it to the other participant in the adjacent room. Of those participants who identified themselves as morally and ethically conscious in their questionnaire at the start of the experiment, the outcome of this experiment (an usually high number of head tosses) proves that their actions contradicted their thoughts.

In similarity to Leonard Bickman's 1972 experiment, our moral framework and the strength we believe we adhere to more often than not contradicts our behaviours. In this example, it was to the tune of 90%.

Principles of persuasion at work:

Although there are no principles of persuasion at work in this experiment, it does highlight that the more traditional form of data analysis to help shape our advertising and marketing approach is somewhat outdated.

If we only look at the geographic and demographic data and attitudes associated with them, it fails to take account of prospective customer's personalities. To have an impact on influencing someone, we need to pay much closer attention to their actual behaviours and consider the O.C.E.A.N 5-point personality model, and then tailor our approach to influence and persuasion accordingly.

This is one of the reasons why it's important in today's technological revolution to collate data about people's personalities from as many sources as possible. We leave a personality residue on all forms of technology we interact with as most request personal information or record it. When it comes to influencing someone's behaviours, we can analyze personality types from set-top box viewing data, social media usage, and online shopping behaviours.

However, it is also worth noting that influencing teenagers or young adults can present a bit of a 'hot potato' as they are more likely to have rebellious tendencies against requests that they feel infringe on their liberties.

This is no more apparent than in the 1999 national anti-smoking campaign that was promoted in America with the tagline of - 'Talk. They'll listen'. This particular ad campaign was targeted at 8th, 9th, and 10th graders. The young adults that these ads were targeted at displayed their rebellious tendencies against the authority, telling them 'not to smoke' by continuing to do so. In fact, a study conducted by the American Journal of Public Health showed that for each additional ad viewed aimed at children, this resulted in a three percent stronger intention to smoke. Between the late 1990s and 2004, US congress assigned almost 1 billion dollars to fund an anti-drug use campaign. Much like the previous example, these ads failed to persuade young adults not to smoke marijuana but have actually encouraged it.

An initial evaluation would suggest that this ad didn't work, but when you consider it was a tobacco-company sponsored ad, you may begin to think its ineffectiveness was beneficial to the sales of the tobacco companies that sponsored it.

Perhaps by understanding the influence triggers behind certain adverts, they could promote an anti-smoking campaign to make it appear as though they were contributing to society by voicing a message of anti-smoking. However, in reality, they were using this principle of persuasion in reverse to their own advantage.

EXPERIMENT 31

The question:

Would you be more likely to reply to a letter or email if the sender had the same first name as you?

YES / NO

The experiment:

In 2005, Randy Garner from Sam Houston State University set out to understand how persuasive similarity is as a principle of persuasion.[49] With the question posed above in mind as the basis for their experiment, Garner and his team of researchers posted out a series of surveys to participants. They varied the names on the cover sheet so that they either matched or did not match the researcher. So, for example, if the participant's name was Thomas Smith, they may receive their correspondence from a researcher called Thomas Green. A non-matching name example would be correspondence addressed to Jane Stevens from a researcher called Lucy Ball. The researchers wanted to determine what the response rate would be based on the similarity of their names.

Garner and his team found the response rate from participants with a name the same as the researchers was around 56%, whilst the non-matching name participants replied to their correspondence letters a mere 30% of the time.

Principles of persuasion at work:

This experiment falls into the likeability principle of persuasion. Creating a connection with somebody can be as simple as sharing the same date of birth, favourite movie, or in this case, the same first name. I would add it is ethically wrong to manufacture a similarity to create a connection, but it is worth being aware that having a similarity with someone can increase your ability to influence them.

EXPERIMENT 32

The question:

Is your mood influenced by the temperature?

YES / NO

The experiment:

Whilst we are all generally happier when we are on our holidays in sunnier climates, this may be due to the fact that we are taking a break from work, in a new place (perhaps more luxurious than home) and on top of that, are enjoying the warmth from the sun. It's in these times of relaxation which place people in a good mood, where people have been influenced into buying a time share, a sombrero, or playing chase the lady with a street hustler thinking we can win. But is it just a holiday that can make us lower our guard and be more easily influenced, or is it temperature too?

This quirky concept has been addressed by a couple of psychologists with Lawrence Williams of Colorado University, suggesting that by making people feel warmer, you could, in fact, make them feel more friendly as a result. In turn, this could potentially mean that they could be more easily influenced if others perceive them as more friendly.

To test this theory, Williams invited participants to his research lab, where they were met by one of his research team.[50] Going up in the lift together, the member of the research team showed the participant that he had his hands full of textbooks and his clipboard and asked the participant if he'd mind holding his warm cup of coffee. Half of the participants were asked to hold a warm cup of coffee, and the other half were asked to hold an iced cup of coffee.

After the participants exited the lift and arrived at the research lab, they were asked to fill out a questionnaire that had a description of a 'Person A'. He was described as intelligent, skilful, industrious, determined, practical, and cautious. The participants were then requested to rate this person's personality. They found that those participants that had held the warm cup of coffee and were asked to read the description of 'Person A' perceived them as much friendlier than those who had held the cup of iced coffee.

On post-evaluation of the experiment, the researchers considered that there might have been some involvement of some kind by the researcher who gave the participant the drink, so they conducted a similar experiment, this time eliminating the involvement of a researcher.

In this second experiment, another group of participants arrived at the lab and then collected their questionnaires. 50% of the participants were then told to pick up and examine a hot therapeutic pad, and the other 50% to pick up and examine a cold therapeutic pad. These pads were picked up by themselves without the interference of a researcher under the guise that they are doing some market research for a range of new therapeutic pads.

After they had completed their questionnaires, as a thank you for taking part, the participants had a choice of reward gift. They could choose either a drink or a $1 gift certificate for their local ice cream shop. Not only that, but the gifts could either be a gift for themselves or gifted to one of their friends.

The researchers found that 75% of the participants primed with the physical coldness from the pads were more likely to choose the gift for themselves and 25% as a gift for their friend. Conversely, 54% of participants who were primed with the physical warmth of the pad were more likely to choose the gift for a friend and 46% more likely to choose a gift for themselves.

In the same year as Leonard Williams and his team were conducting their experiments, so too was Chen-Bo Zhong from North Western University in America. Zhong recognized that warmth was closely linked to social inclusion from the start of our lives, where we are embraced by our parents and made to feel warm. Warmth is also associated with security, open fires, and we hear the phrase 'warm personality' or 'I'm warming to it'.

Conversely, phrases such as 'being frozen out', 'icy stare' 'cold and callous behaviour' are colder and less friendly traits. Zhong and her team embarked on a simple study in which she invited a handful of participants to the lab.[51] 50% were asked to think about a time when they had been rejected by others and remember it in vivid detail, including the temperature. The other 50% were asked to think of a time when they had been accepted as part of a group, and again, remember it in vivid detail, and estimate the temperature.

As per Zhong's original assumptions, those that thought about a time when they were alone described that they felt significantly colder than those who had described a time when they had been accepted as part of a group.

Principles of persuasion at work:

Whilst there are no principles of persuasion at work here, the experiments above suggest that people are a lot more friendly and malleable to be influenced if they both experience warmth or physically feel warm. So, if you are attempting to influence somebody, make sure you do so in a warm room or environment, or lend them your jacket if they are cold, also employing reciprocity as a principle of persuasion.

EXPERIMENT 33

The question:

Earlier, we looked at how a puzzle written on the top of your receipt may subtly persuade you to tip the waiter a little more than you had originally intended to.

Could this same principle of persuasion work if the gift was more tangible, like a sweet as an example?

Would it be even more persuasive if the waiter gave you two sweets with your bill?

Would you like him the most if he gave you one sweet and then, as an afterthought, gave you an extra sweet?

The experiment:

This similar study to the experiment involving the numbers of Fs in a particular sentence is once again conducted by David Strohmetz and his research team.[52] They wanted to determine what effect giving sweets with the bill at the end of a meal has on the number of tips left for the waiter or waitress.

Much like his earlier experiment, this was simple in its structure but profound in its results.

Upon presenting the bill to the diner, the researcher posing as a waiter left them a single sweet. In doing so, Strohmetz and his team noticed a modest 3.3% increase in the value of tips left compared to the value of tips given if no sweet was left. They repeated the process, this time with the waiter leaving two sweets to accompany the diner's bill. This time they found that the value of tips had increased to 14.1% compared to no sweets left. Both of these reflect the underpinning ideas behind the principle of reciprocity in that if you give something to someone, they will feel obliged to give something back in return. In this case, the waiter gave a sweet as a gift to the diner, and as a result, they felt obligated to give something in return, in this instance, a tip of varying amounts.

Where this experiment really made a splash was when the waiter gave the diner just one sweet and then turned to leave, reconsidered his departure, and gave them another sweet saying, "oh for you nice people". This resulted in an astonishing 23% increase in tip value compared to the average tip left by someone receiving no sweets.

Principles of persuasion at work:

This experiment emphasizes the power of reciprocity as a principle of persuasion and reiterates the three factors that make a gift or a favour more persuasive and, therefore, more likely to be reciprocated.

The first contributing factor is that the gift should be significant. Whilst an increase from 1 to 2 sweets is not a big difference, it is double the giving of just one sweet and, therefore, comparatively significant. Significance should not represent the financial worth of the gift or favour but the impact it has on the other person.

The second contributing factor is the way that the gift or favour should be given. The most persuasive way is giving the gift when someone least expects it. If the gift or favour becomes expected, the receiver becomes numb to the gesture, and it doesn't carry the same persuasive weight.

Finally, the gift or favour should be personalized. In this particular example, the extra sweet was given as an afterthought, with the underlying connotation being that it was given because the waiter was particularly fond of the diners and did not generally give an extra sweet to everyone.

Regardless of whether the situation to give an extra sweet (favour or an alternative gift) is contrived or not, the gift should be given with authenticity. Not only that, but the focus should not be on the value of the gift given but on the way it is given. If an extra sweet was given to all diners on all the tables, then the reciprocity principle will collapse because the diners may see that the sweet is no longer personalized. Instead, they will perceive the sweet as expected if they see others having one (or two), and it loses its' significance for them. The authenticity is lost.

Although the gift or favour does not have to be expensive, it should be one that has been considered and the most suitable for the receiver. Whilst the offering of a free shot of Limoncello is a nice gesture at the end of a diner's Italian meal is nice, if the diners have not been drinking all evening, a pot of herbal tea may be of the same value but be more tailored to them.

EXPERIMENT 34

The question:

Are you more heavily influenced if you are given something extra for free at the end of a negotiation in an attempt to encourage you to buy that particular product or service?

The experiment:

In 1986, psychologist Jerry Burger examined the effectiveness of a compliance procedure known as the 'That's-not-all technique'.[53] He conducted seven experiments with 426 young adults, undergraduates, and adults to examine the effectiveness of this technique. This technique involves offering a product or service at a high price, not allowing the prospective customer to respond for a few seconds, and then adding another product or service for free or offering a discount on the original item.

Burger's experiment involved him and his team selling cupcakes. In the first experiment, he sold one cupcake with two cookies together for 75 cents to 50% of the shoppers. This acted as the control. To the other 50% of shoppers, he sold one cupcake but then added two cookies 'for free', applying the 'that's not all technique'.

Burger found that 40% of sales were made through the control, whilst a far higher 73% of customers bought the cupcake when he used the 'that's-not-all technique' and threw in the extra cookies for free.

In Burger's second experiment, he demonstrated a different application of his 'that's-not-all technique'. Here he attempted to sell the cupcakes for 75 cents, with no additional cookies to 50% of his customers. This represented the control. To the other 50% of his potential customers, he priced the cupcakes at $1 each and then immediately discounted them to 75 cents. 44% of shoppers in his control group bought a cupcake, whist 73% of customers bought a cupcake when he applied the 'That-not-all technique' once again demonstrating its effectiveness.

Principles of persuasion at work:

Reciprocation and likeability are evident principles of persuasion here. These two principles of persuasion often go arm in arm because people like others who have given them something for free, especially if it is personalized. In these experiments, the prospective customers felt an increasing obligation to purchase the product in return for the salesperson's 'concessions' with each incremental addition of a 'bonus' product or service.

Applying this powerful influence technique depends largely on an automatic social response. As a result, it can work better when the customer does not have time to think for long about the situation. Applying this when selling a product or service, you can add extra 'bonus gifts' to a product offering or start with a high price and gradually come down. The most effective approach is to tell them all the additional benefits you are going to give them all at one time. Whilst the incremental concessions should make the proposition ever more appealing, this technique has an even greater level of persuasiveness if the final increment is particularly desirable.

EXPERIMENT 35

The question:

Could you be influenced to act in a way that you didn't necessarily agree with if you first found yourself in a role play position, or do you think it would have no effect on your beliefs?

IT WOULD AFFECT YOU / IT WOULD HAVE NO EFFECT ON YOU

The experiment:

In 1966, American psychologist Alan Elms set out to explore the idea that if people acted as though they believed in a certain argument, they would change their own attitudes and beliefs in favour of the attitude they were asked to support.[54] More succinctly put - was it possible to encourage somebody to influence themselves to change their own beliefs.

In a number of experiments that concentrated on modifying the smoking habits of people, Elms and his team invited several participants to his lab to play the role of lung cancer patients and split them into two groups. In the first group, another participant played the role of the doctor sharing bad news about the deterioration of their condition to the participants.

In the second group, the participants simply received the information about their deteriorating condition by listening to a recording of the role-playing session. The role-playing group showed markedly greater changes in attitudes than those who had simply listened to the recording.

In a similar experiment, cigarette smokers were asked to play the role of non-smokers and to attempt to convince other smokers to quit. Their roles were assigned randomly. The participants were assigned to either role-play giving the persuasive argument or actively listening to these arguments. Much like the previous study, Elms and his team found that, again, the role players showed a significantly greater attitude change than those simply listening. Some of the role-players even made a greater attitude change over time too, when the researchers revisited them.

Several other studies have involved a similar process involving political views too. Participants, who role-played giving political speeches for a party that they weren't necessarily in favour of, noticed an attitudinal change more in favour of them and realized that this party wasn't as bad as they had first perceived.

All of these examples show just how powerful taking part in a role-play can have on influencing someone's ingrained beliefs, which months of targeted marketing and advertising cannot even change.

As mentioned earlier in the book, by collating information on people's actions, it is this data that can be used far more effectively than just a 'one size fits all' form of marketing or influence technique. Perhaps the most striking example of where we can see behaviours and actions change through role play is in the notorious 1973 Stanford Prison Experiment conducted by Philip Zimbardo and his team.[55] In this experiment, a group of students was assigned roles of either a prison guard or prisoner. Despite personality assessments conducted before the test, attesting that all 24 prisoners and guards were both mentally and physically stable, the experiment had to be abandoned after just six days due to the emotional breakdowns of the prisoners caused by excessive aggression of the guards who took on their characters far too seriously.

Principles of persuasion at work:

All of the above experiments demonstrate consensus as the principle of persuasion. In our lives, most of the things we do, we do with a high degree of consistency. Specifically, our thoughts and actions should be in unison. Much like the role plays conducted with smokers, Zimbardo's Stanford prison experiment revealed how people would readily conform to the social roles they are expected to play.[56] This emphasizes again that it is the behaviours that are exhibited that can contribute to high levels of self-influence. Again, this reiterates the importance of considering people's core behaviours just as much as their attitudes, beliefs, demographic and geographic data.

EXPERIMENT 36

The question:

Would you class yourself as charismatic? Whether your answer is yes, or no, would you describe yourself as having a particularly emotive face?

YES / NO

The experiment:

Throughout history, it has been the most charismatic leaders who have generally been able to influence the most people. Leaders such as Mahatma Gandhi, Martin Luther King, Fidel Castro, Winston Churchill, Adolf Hitler, and Eva Peron were all charismatic communicators who were able to bypass people's thought processes and make them 'feel'. By doing so, they were able to influence them much more effectively by speaking to their heart.

All of the leaders above can be described as being both verbally expressive and also facially expressive. A number of studies conducted by psychologists Elaine Hatfield, Milton Friedman, and Marc Andreessen looked at whether emotional empathy is sensitive to facial feedback and also whether people can be influenced through exposure to non-verbal clues.[57]

To test the latter of the two theories Hatfield and her colleagues split participants into two groups, with one expressive person and two un-expressive people in small groups. In their groups of three, the participants sat facing one another for 2 minutes without speaking. The subsequent questionnaire completed by both the expressive and un-expressive people revealed that whilst the feelings of the un-expressive participants had been influenced by those more expressive participants, this had not been reciprocated the other way. In this case, the expressive people felt no change in emotion. This demonstrates the clear power of non-verbal communication and the influential effect it can have over others even when we aren't aware of it.[58]

The second study conducted by psychologists Per Andreasson and Ulf Dimberg in 2008 studied whether empathy is related to the sensitivity of facial feedback.[59] One hundred and twelve participants were invited to the lab and asked to complete a questionnaire to score their own levels of emotional empathy and charisma. With this data, they were then split into two groups, one group having high levels of empathy and the other group having low levels of empathy.

Throughout the experiment, the facial expressions of each group were then manipulated into either happy or sad expressions, and at the same time, the participants watched humorous movies. The participants then rated these movies to the degree of humour they felt. The study found that there was "a significant interaction between empathy and condition". The participants who were identified as having high empathy and charisma rated the films as being funnier in a happy condition than those who were deemed as having low levels of empathy. They also had a greater tendency to find the movies less funny when their facial expressions when manipulated into a sulky condition compared to the high empathy group. By taking these findings into account, it can be concluded that the more highly empathetic a person, the greater degree to which they mimic the emotions of the environment around them in this example, the comedy movies manifested themselves as humour. This can be equally applied to sadness and pain. By experiencing the emotions of those around us, our personality becomes much more authentic, allowing us to connect with greater ease with others, leading to the greater chance that any negotiations will result in a win-win outcome.

Principles of persuasion at work:

Here we see how powerful the likability principle of persuasion is. It has been shown time and time again that by connecting with others in an authentic, understanding, and empathetic way, it allows one to be much more influential in negotiations. As with any negotiation, placing the prospective client first and being empathetic and authentic allows you to truly understand what problem they have and how you or your company can offer the solution. We all mimic facial expressions and body language around us, and it happens more naturally when we authentically connect with others. Mimicking others' facial expressions and body movements can also be practised to simulate a greater connection than we perhaps may have at the outset of an interaction. In Neuro-Linguistic Programming terminology, this is called 'mirroring'. Mirroring occurs in social situations or with friends and family and is most noticeable when they smile you smile back. You can also observe this when someone yawns. Involuntarily, you find yourself yawning too. You may also find yourself sitting or standing in the same pose or position as somebody, and again this builds connections much more rapidly. Emotions are extremely powerful and even contagious, and a smile can pass from one person to another and soon can have the whole room smiling. This process has evolved to promote group empathy and cohesion and to give charismatic presenters the edge in situations of influence.

EXPERIMENT 37

The question:

Based on your ever-increasing knowledge about influence, how would you help resolve a situation in a school which has become overwhelmed with fear, suspicion, and distrust between racial groups in the classroom and resulted in hostile classroom atmospheres and has seen a recent spike in fist-fights and violence?

The experiment:

In 1971, University of Texas psychologist Elliot Aronson was contacted by a local school superintendent who explained the situation above and asked if Elliot could help diffuse the situation and apply his skills to encourage the children to get on with one another.[60] The explosive situation was the result of traditionally desegregated children being all put in the same classroom together for the first time. Cultures ranged from white to African American to Hispanic children.

Aronson included his own undergraduate students he had been teaching in the resolution and treated it as a case study. When Aronson and his team arrived at the school, their first observation was that the inter-group hostility was, in part, being fuelled by the competitive environment of the classroom. This was apparent in many classrooms where the teacher poses a question, and those who know the answer raise their hand, those that don't, don't. It left some feeling stupid whilst others felt smug. This competitive environment needed to be redesigned to one which focussed more on co-operation.

In order to combat this situation, Aronson and his team of undergraduates devised and implemented what they called 'The Jigsaw Method'.

The next subject on the curriculum for the fifth-grade class was for the students to learn about the biography of Eleanor Roosevelt. Rather than using the traditional competitive method of asking the students to answer questions that they may or may not know, Aronson divided the students into highly diversified groups irrespective of race, age, ethnic background, or gender. Each student was then assigned one particular part of Roosevelt's biography to learn, and then the group would be collectively assessed. This meant that those students who came from underfunded schools and substandard neighbourhoods, which may have reduced their academic ability, were now in a group where some of the more academic students were able to help them to ensure the group collectively passed the exam. With this approach implemented, instead of classroom culture fuelled by competition, the dynamic of these groups was now fuelled by cooperation and collaboration. This meant that those students who were usually too shy to put their hands up through lack of confidence were now involved in the learning process.

When one of Aronson's undergraduate team overhead some nasty bullying within one of the groups, she reiterated the importance of co-operation so that they can all collectively pass their exams and that bullying or a lack of co-operation could cost them the chance to excel in their exams. As a result of interventions like these, the classroom culture changed from being inhospitable to much more humane. Overall the stereotypes began to change, and absenteeism from the class went down. Of note was one boy called Carlos, who had poor levels of English. When he was placed in a group with classmates who had at one time ostracised him due to his poor English and different background, he now found himself being helped with both his presentation and speaking skills by those same members of his group.

As with all credible experiments, Aronson also deployed his innovative Jigsaw Method to some classrooms and not others to act as control groups. Again, he found that compared to the classes where his method had not been implemented, there was found to be less prejudice and negative stereotyping, and the students themselves found that they enjoyed attending school better and felt more confident. Other side-effects of this method included an improvement in the student's overall academic abilities and school absenteeism declined. Compared to the control group classrooms, the teachers who were working with the Jigsaw Method found that their students were achieving better results than those classrooms which had not experienced the Jigsaw Method intervention.

Principles of persuasion at work:

It is the consensus principle of persuasion that we find at play here. This principle encourages the individuals to follow the group to work in harmony. Similarly, the Jigsaw Method is a tried and tested, proven technique to influence children to put aside their racial and background differences and work in harmony to achieve a collaborative goal.

EXPERIMENT 38

The question:

Is it possible to influence a student to perform at a higher level educationally just by encouraging them to believe they are naturally attuned to becoming a high achiever?

YES / NO

The experiment:

The 'Pygmalion effect' is known as the phenomenon whereby others' expectations of a target person affects the target person's performance.

In 1968, psychologist Robert Rosenthal and his colleague, Lenore Jacobson set out to determine whether the Pygmalion effect was applicable to students in a school environment.[61] He wanted to understand if it was possible to influence the ability of a child simply by increasing the expectation of them.

To conduct the experiment, Rosenthal and Jacobson tested the IQ of students at a local school using the Tests of General Ability (TOGA). This particular assessment was chosen because the teachers were unlikely to be familiar with it. As a result, the psychologists were able to manipulate the results for the second part of the experiment. This second stage involved Rosenthal and Jacobson choosing the students who had taken part in the assessment at random and identifying them as the top 20% performers in the test. They then shared these names with the 18 teachers and waited till the end of the year to return to school to evaluate any changes. On their return, Rosenthal and Jacobson gave all the students, including those who had not been randomly identified as 'blooming', another IQ test using the same TOGA format for consistency.

They found there was a marked difference in IQ score tests. The students who had been randomly identified as 'ready to bloom' or high achievers showed greater gains (to an average of 15 points on their IQ test) than those who had not, despite these names being chosen at random.

The results of this experiment demonstrate both the power of a self-fulfilling prophecy in that the students who were told they were on the verge of academic success performed in accordance with these expectations. Similarly, what may have had a more powerful impact on their increased IQ test was the influence from the teachers who had higher expectations of them too.

In 1988, Gary Wells from Iowa University also found that the Pygmalion theory could even lead police officers to un-intentionally influence witnesses to incorrectly identify certain suspects from a line-up.[62] It was only when researchers told the witnesses that they didn't have to choose a suspect from the line-up that they were presented with that this reduced the numbers of false identification. That simple instruction ensured that the witnesses' ability to make accurate identifications was less clouded.

Principles of persuasion at work:

The Pygmalion effect is a nuance in behavioural psychology itself, and as such, there are no principles of persuasion at work here. The above experiments demonstrate that it is possible to influence somebody's performance simply by having higher or lower expectations of them.

EXPERIMENT 39

The question:

Do you think that the power of influence can be so strong at times that you could be influenced into plunging your hand into a beaker of acid?

YES / NO

The experiment:

This experiment starts with quite an eye-brow-raising question. It could, perhaps, have been preceded by a question enquiring as to whether you believe in hypnosis or not, and if you do, whether you think you would be susceptible to it?

Hypnosis is a human condition that involves a 'hypnotist' focussing the participants' attention, reducing their peripheral awareness, and ultimately enhancing their capacity to respond to a suggestion or series of suggestions. In its most simplified form – hypnosis is a word given to enhanced levels of suggestibility (or influence). Hypnosis is generally more successful for those who are open to suggestion. To identify the most suggestable participants, hypnotists usually start any performance with a number of participants performing 'set pieces'. This is where the body's natural mechanism contributes to the outcome of the instruction under the guise of hypnosis.

Let's try. The first experiment is perhaps the most traditional in the arsenal of a hypnotist.

Stand with your arms bent at 90 degrees and the palms of your hands together. Apply pressure to the palms of your hands and then interlace your fingers as though you are making a plea to god. Now extend your two forefingers, keeping your palms together and fingers and thumbs interlaced, but keep your fingers apart. Once you have done this, focus all of your attention on the gap in between your two fingers and imagine a small magnet on the pad of your index finger. Imagine that these two magnets are pulling each other together, and the more you notice it, the stronger it gets. The more you focus, the more the magnetic pull will become stronger, and the more your fingers move, the closer your fingers will move together. Keep focussing. In a few moments, you will feel your fingers meet.

If this is delivered with the correct authority, tonality, and direction, you will find that most people's fingers will come together. This is predominantly based on human physiology, but it also allows a hypnotist to eliminate those participants with who this does not work with.

These are the people who are potentially not open to suggestion and, as a result, try and prevent the natural physiology of the body from working. Once you have eliminated these people, if you were then to perform a few other set pieces with less dependence on the physiology and more dependence on suggestion and influence, you would soon eliminate even more of the lesser suggestible participants until you are left with one who you will be able to 'hypnotize' into performing unbelievable acts that even they didn't think were possible. Place the psychological principle of 'social influence' into the mix, and the participant will start acting in ways that they think are appropriate for a hypnotized figure to act and, voila, you have a credible, open subject to work with.

In an experiment conducted by Martin Orne and Frederick Evans in 1965, they followed a similar process and found a particularly malleable subject.[63] Through 'hypnosis', the participant picked up a piece of chalk, a harmless reptile, a coin, a venomous snake, and then finally plunged their hand into a beaker of acid. The participant was left unharmed as the researchers had switched out the acid for a beaker of water. It was a good thing, too, because as soon as the researchers explained the experiment, the participant threw the acid at them.

After the experiment, the participant agreed that they would never do such a thing in their regular waking state. There were a couple of reasons for the participant's compliance with all the instructions given to him. Firstly, he previously acknowledged that he was in a controlled laboratory setting. With this knowledge in mind, it gives him the confidence that the researchers would not let any harm come to him, which can be described as 'social influence'. Secondly, and perhaps the most relevant for the purpose of this experiment, was that he was more inclined to behave in a certain way because he had initially been selected due to his general suggestibility and openness.

Whilst it could be argued that the participants were simply pretending to be hypnotized and act in ways they think a hypnotized person should, Orne and Evans continued with a second stage of the experiment to eliminate this possibility.[64] In this second stage, they chose 6 participants who had not passed the first round of 'set-pieces' or were deemed to be the least suggestible of the original group. They asked them to merely pretend to be hypnotized and pick up the non-venomous snake first and then the venomous snake. All complied with both requests in the same way as those who were actually 'hypnotized'.

When, they too, were debriefed after the experiment and asked why they had followed both instructions, the same as the hypnotized participants, again, they believed that no harm would come to them because not only did the University ethics committee not allow them to be placed in dangerous situations, but if the researchers had contravened this rule, they had faith that the experiment was being conducted by competent and reliable scientists.

Principles of persuasion at work:

To influence somebody to plunge their hand into a beaker of acid requires a specific environment for this to work. The process to arrive at this one participant is not always covered in behavioural psychology books, but all forms of professional hypnotism follow this format. Perhaps the most powerful influencer here is the researcher. The participants believe that no harm will come to them and, as a result, allow themselves to be influenced by placing their trust in an authoritative figure. Thus, authority is the principle of persuasion at work in this situation.

EXPERIMENT 40

The question:

Do you have a prophecy of the world? It doesn't have to be something you have shared with anyone, perhaps simply internalized. Your prophecy might be:

'Climate change won't really affect us all that bad, and the world will eventually heal itself'.

What happens if your prophecy about the world didn't come true and the by-products of climate change had an increasingly destructive effect on the planet. It could be this example or another example where one of your core beliefs is one day proved completely inaccurate or incorrect?

The experiment:

In 1954, psychologist Leon Festinger (of cognitive dissonance acclaim) and his colleagues Henry Riecken and Stanley Schachter infiltrated a cult that believed the end of the world was only two months away.[65] They wanted to answer the questions posed above: How would the members of the cult feel if this prophecy was not fulfilled? Would they admit to the error of their prophecy, or would they readjust their reality to make sense of the new circumstance where their prophecy had not come true?

The cult in question was led by a Chicago housewife called Dorothy Martin or, for the purpose of the study, known by her alias Marian Keech.

Keech had supposedly received a prophecy via automatic writing from aliens on the planet Clarion telling her that the world was going to end with a great flood before dawn on the 21st December 1954. She had shared with prophecy with others and, in doing so, had convinced 11 people that this prophecy was going to come true. In blind belief, some left their jobs, college, spouses, and some had even given away their money and possessions. She had claimed these would not be needed when a flying saucer would come and rescue them.

Keech had also been told, again via automatic writing, that the aliens would knock on her door before midnight and escort them to a nearby spaceship. They had also advised her that all of her party would need to remove anything magnetic before they could be whisked away on the spaceship. Just before midnight, the group met at Keech's house and removed bar straps, jewellery, belt buckles, cut the eyelets from their shoes, and zips from their trousers and jackets. At 1205am, no one had arrived. One of the groups noticed that another clock said 11.55 pm, so the group waited. In fact, they waited until 4 am at which point Keech started to cry. At 4.45 am, she then received another message via automatic writing to say that God had decided to save the planet from destruction because the group had spread so much light on the earth.

With no visit from aliens, and no flood, and calling into question the authenticity of Keech's claims, of the eleven group members, only two decided to leave. The other members, who had previously been so reluctant to give interviews, and had such a distaste for the media, then embarked on an urgent campaign, spreading this new message as far and wide as possible. Eventually, the remaining members of the group also went their separate ways, and Keech went into hiding. A few years before her death, she reappeared, saying that she was still in contact with aliens.

Principles of persuasion at work:

Consensus, authority, and commitment are the principles of persuasion at work here, with the 11 members of her group following Keech as the authoritative leader. Keech also uses the 'foot-in-the-door' technique in which her group agrees to smaller actions (such as joining her group, attending a meeting, etc.) before finally giving up their jobs, money, and even their spouses. The consensus principle combined with 'foot-in-the-door-technique' used to influence others is not solely constrained to cult members.

In similarity to the group members who bought into Keech's prophecy and then justified the unrealized prophecy, marketers also apply a similar principle. In advertising, the self-justification principle is used to encourage people to pay more for a product and justify their purchase if they feel buyer's remorse. Furthermore, we may find ourselves recommending the products or services we bought to our friends and family to justify the purchases ourselves, especially if they are expensive.

We also see politicians using these techniques to silence dissenting voices and opposition to their actions and manifesto and equally misdirect people away from the true facts, figures, and intent behind their actions.

Festinger's further analysis of the study suggested that there must be five conditions present if somebody is to become an even more passionate believer after a failure of disconfirmation. These conditions also have strong ties with influence and self-influence:

1. The belief that the person holds must be congruent with what they do or how they behave. So, if they believe that the environment is in decline unless we stop burning fossil fuels, they wouldn't use transport that made use of these fuels or even protest against the digging of oil wells.
2. The person holding the belief must have committed themselves to it and have taken some action that is difficult to undo (such as giving away all your money or divorcing your spouse). The greater the action and more difficult they are to undo, the greater the individual's commitment to the belief and the greater ease they are to be influenced.
3. The belief must be sufficiently specific and sufficiently concerned with the real world so that events may unequivocally refute the belief.
4. Any dis-confirmatory evidence that occurs must be recognized by the individual holding the belief
5. The individual must have social support to help maintain any beliefs that may be challenged by non-believers.

EXPERIMENT 41

The question:

Imagine you were in a forest, and you see some brilliantly coloured minerals and stones around you in the ground, which have been preserved in the form of logs and stumps. You are tempted to take one home with you, and then you see this sign:

"Your heritage is being vandalized every day by theft losses of petrified wood of fourteen tons a year, mostly a small piece at a time."

Would this make you less likely to take the wood chip?

YES / NO

The experiment:

The Petrified Forest in northeastern Arizona is home to the aforementioned brilliantly coloured minerals, and stones persevered in the form of logs and stumps. The park had been experiencing high levels of theft, so in 2006, they sought the assistance of the prominent psychologist, Robert Cialdini, to help them curb these thefts.[66]

If your answer to the question above was 'yes', then that is similar to many other people's thoughts, but in reality, it didn't help at all.

The statement above was a sign that had been placed in the Petrified

Forest but was failing to make a positive impact on the level of theft. The sign communicates both factual information and highlights the fact that other people are also stealing or vandalizing the forest. It also makes the assumption that we are rational people and make information-based decisions. However, it doesn't account for the fact that, in reality, we generally don't.

Having seen the sign, which was failing to achieve the desired effect, Cialdini and his team spent the next five weeks erecting two differently worded signs on the footpaths around the park and monitored peoples' behaviours. For the first sign, he used an injunctive norm form of message. It offered a loose guideline on how to behave and an image of a shady character (Cialdini himself) stealing from the forest but with a big red circle and bar over the hands. The request read:

"Please don't remove the petrified wood chip".

The second sign followed a more descriptive norm form of a message suggesting that:

"Many visitors have removed the petrified wood chip from the park, changing the state of the Petrified Forest".

Of these two signs, the first one had the most impact, with less than 2% of the wood chips being taken!

It still didn't prevent the thefts entirely, because as humans, we often dismiss guidelines of how to behave. For example, if we are told to obey the speed limit, we occasionally drive faster. If we are encouraged to eat our fruit and vegetables to remain fit and healthy, now and again, we will opt for some junk food. Finally, if we see a no-smoking sign, we might light up a cigarette, regardless.

The second sign, which was written in a more descriptive norm style, in fact, had the opposite effect on visitors, and it was found that there was a four-fold increase (or 8%) in the amount taken. In fact, this was even worse than the control areas where no signs were erected. These reported a 2.92% increase in the level of theft.

One of the main reasons for the second sign leading to an increase in the number of petrified wood chips being taken is the statement normalizing the behaviour that it was trying to prevent. In effect, it made it sound normal to steal the wood chip.[67]

Despite the compelling evidence, the park administrators refused to change their counter-productive signs, yet the evidence was so strong this principle has since been referenced as the 'Petrified Wood Principle' and is critical to consider if you are thinking about any form of communication or advertising aimed at changing or influencing behaviour.

The Petrified Wood Principle is used to inspire people to consider their naturally compulsive actions more consciously through the power of communal affiliation. However, even when we know this and the evidence supports experiments, as in the case of the Petrified Wood Forest, we still have an innate belief that we can influence people's behaviour through logic and information-led reasoning even when the evidence above contradicts it.

Principles of persuasion at work:

Social proof is the principle of persuasion at work here. With this principle, we look to what others do or have done to inform our own decisions. However, you can see that communicating what others have done or do can actually have a destructive effect as well as a constructive effect depending on the norms conveyed.

By simply communicating what certain kind of behavior is disapproved of, without providing any facts or figures on what the majority are doing, this can have a more negative effect than if this data were included.

In situations where you are attempting to influence or modify behaviour, it's important to focus on what the majority is doing. In the experiment outlined above, before Cialdini arrived, 97% of visitors were not stealing from the forest, so those that were were in the minority. The signs they had at the time could have been further improved by reframing the statistics in this way. This approach would have encouraged the visitors to focus on the positive behaviour of others and would have been a much more influential persuasion technique. If you curate a statement that both disapproves of the behaviour of the minority and encourages the behaviour of the majority, this can supercharge the persuasive message in your sign, advert, piece of creative or personal approach to influence.

For example, if you are experiencing late comers at work, the most effective way to apply this approach is to approve and appreciate those who are punctual but equally disapprove of those who are late. Whilst this may have a small impact on those who arrive on time and may then want to adjust their behaviours to fit with what they think are the social norms of arriving late, those who arrive late will see the social norm of arriving on time and move towards that. Overall, this approach will have a much more effective result than simply disapproving of those who arrive late.

EXPERIMENT 42

The question:

Do you value a free gift as much as a gift that you paid for if both of them are exactly the same?

YES / NO

The experiment:

In 2004, social scientist Priya Raghubir wanted to evaluate whether a bonus gift you receive as an added extra for purchasing a standalone item has the same perceived value and desirability as a standalone item by itself.[68] To investigate this, Raghubir invited several participants to read a duty-free catalogue where a bottle of alcohol was the target product, and a pearl bracelet was the bonus item.

Raghubir split the participants into two groups and asked the first to assign a value to the add-on gift and the second group to value the pearl bracelet as a standalone gift. Those who valued the pearl bracelet as an add-on gift said they would be 35% less likely to purchase it than those who saw it as a standalone item.

The reason for this lower valuation is perhaps the result of any internal dialogue of the participants asking themselves whether the item had been discontinued in the past, is obsolete, or is an older model or style.

Thus, it is essential to remind potential customers about the true value of what they may be getting as a free or bonus gift. For example, rather than describing a book, you are giving away as free, it is much better to describe it as a book 'which is valued at $15.99 but will cost you nothing'. By doing so, this communicates the true value of the offer.

Influencing people to take advantage of this offer alongside their purchase is not solely resigned to products. The communication message can be equally applied to services too. As an example, in the business world, if you are going to assist a colleague just before you go home, communicating that you will be happy to spend an hour with them because you appreciate how much they need to complete a particular project, communicates the value of your additional hour much more than saying nothing.

Principles of persuasion at work:

An inverted version of the scarcity principle of persuasion is evident here. The principle of scarcity suggests that the less available the resource, the more we want it. In this example, however, the bracelet is being given away as a free gift which devalues not only the gift itself but also the item that it is associated with. When something is added as a bonus item, everyone gets one when they make their initial purchase. Rather than the free gift being less available, in this example, it is more available and thus renders it less scarce and, in the example above, resulted in 35% fewer people wanting to purchase it as a standalone gift.

EXPERIMENT 43

The question:

Are you influenced by fear as a motivator for you to take action or change your behaviour?

YES / NO

The experiment:

In 1965, health researcher Howard Leventhal conducted an experiment to understand if fear-based advertising or communication as a method of influence could actually motivate someone into taking action.[69]

Leventhal began his experiment by splitting participants into four different groups and getting each group to read a differently constructed pamphlet detailing tetanus.

The pamphlets were composed of two sections. The first section was focusing on the causes of tetanus and the case history of a tetanus patient, which Leventhal described as the fear section. The second section was a recommendation section that focussed on the importance of being immunized to help prevent the disease. Leventhal and his team produced four forms of these pamphlets, also including a high fear and low fear message as well as specific and non-specific recommendations on how to arrange a tetanus jab. Leventhal also arranged for another pamphlet to be produced to act as a control which contained no warnings about tetanus and no detailed plan on how to get the tetanus jab either.

The result found that those participants who read the high fear pamphlets were the most motivated to take action. However, this was only the case if it included a clear and specific action plan for them on how to get a jab, thereby reducing their fear of tetanus which would have almost certainly caused a paralytic effect on them taking action.

This study can be applied to real-world situations, too - specifically in the world of advertising. If you first communicate the threat posed to the success of a company or industry, then accompany this with specific, actionable steps that the consumer can take to alleviate or resolve the danger or problem.

In advertising, you can influence your target market by eliciting hope that you can help them overcome their problems in one sentence.

To create a persuasive or influential call-to-action, you should start by incorporating the thing that they both desire and fear the most into one sentence starting with 'How to' (do something). This should then be followed by inserting the preposition 'without' in the middle of the sentence. In the example focussed on tetanus, you could use this persuasive formula to write the following:

"How to avoid getting tetanus without wrapping yourself in cotton wool!"

or

"How to prevent the spread of tetanus without ending up in hospital!"

Here, these sentences suggest that the target audience may fear extra caution to prevent them from getting tetanus, or in the second example, if they don't take precautionary measures, they may end up in hospital. The thing that the target audience would want most - is not to get tetanus.

Principles of persuasion at work:

Whilst fear is not classed as a principle of persuasion, it certainly can be persuasive! When applied correctly, it can be extremely influential. Fear does, however, sit under the umbrella of behavioural or personality data alongside the OCEAN model mentioned earlier and the principles of persuasion.

Scaring people using a fear-based approach to influence without providing specific, actionable steps can actually influence the target audience not to take action.

This approach to successful influence can be applied across all sectors of society, including healthcare. For example, if you have a patient who is overweight, it is often not sufficient to explain that they are on course to having a heart attack, cardiovascular disease, or diabetes. There is a high chance that they are already aware of this and have simply 'blocked it out of their mind' as it is their reaction to fear.

Using the approach above, it is more persuasive to explain to the patient about side-effects that may happen if they remain overweight. These suggestions should then be accompanied by a specific plan, which, in this case, would focus on dietary changes and an exercise regime.

EXPERIMENT 44

The question:

Which of the following pieces of office stationery can supercharge your powers of influence?

1. A pen
2. A pencil
3. An eraser
4. A clipboard
5. A Post-it note
6. A coaster
7. A sharpie marker
8. A pen holder
9. An office mascot
10. A note pad

The experiment:

In 2005, social scientist Randy Garner wanted to explore the idea whether sticky notes (sorry if I've given the game away prematurely), also known by their more common name Post-it notes, would increase the compliance with a written request to another person.[70]

The first stage of the experiment was to send out three different surveys with a request for people to complete the one they received. The first batch of surveys had a handwritten Post-it note stuck to the cover letter, which was mailed alongside the survey. The second batch of surveys has the same survey and cover letter, but this time there was no Post-it note attached, but a handwritten message had been scribed onto the cover letter instead. The third batch of surveys, and in this instance, the control group, were simply sent with the cover letter and survey and no additional Post-it note or handwritten note. All three cover letters requested the surveys to be completed and returned to the sender as soon as possible.

The results were remarkable. 75% of the surveys from the first batch were returned that had the handwritten Post-it note on them. 48% of the second batch of surveys were returned. These had the handwritten note scribed onto the cover letter. Finally, 36% of surveys from the last batch were returned that contained no Post-it-note or handwritten message.

Garner and his team evaluated the results and considered that the level of returned versus non-returned surveys could have been due to the vibrant colour of the neon Post-it note, making it stand out more and therefore prompting people to react.

Based on this potential bias, they conducted another experiment with a plain Post-it note with a handwritten request on one-third of the surveys, a plain Post-it note with no message on the other third, whilst the remaining third simply contained just the cover letter and survey. This time, 69% of the surveys with the handwritten Post-it notes attached were returned. 43% of the surveys with the blank Post-it note were returned. Finally, 34% of the surveys with no Post-it note included were returned.

In both experiments, the surveys with the handwritten Post-it notes had not only been returned in a timelier manner, but the rate at which they had been returned was the highest too. Not only that but, the surveys with the handwritten Post-it notes had been completed with more detail and more effort. Later studies showed that this return rate would be even higher still when the researchers wrote thank you on the Post-it note too.

Principles of persuasion at work:

Here we see the reciprocity principle of persuasion at work; this time applied in a slightly different manner. Those who received the handwritten Post-it notes had felt that these had been personalized to them. Not only that, but it was unexpected to have a Post-it note attached to the cover letter explaining the request that they should complete the survey and return. Furthermore, the note also subtly communicates that this is a personalized gift too. As a result, the participant feels more obliged to reciprocate and return the survey completed. The more personalized a gift or favour is, the more likely someone is to agree to any future request.

Applying this in the workplace couldn't be easier. It takes only a few moments to add a Post-it note and write on it, and the visibility of the neon colours may help keep your document or request in the receiver's mind's eye. In our digital age, 'note.ly' is a website where you can create your own digital Post-it notes and send them to people. Personalize it, and you have something unique that the recipients will feel you have gone to an extra effort to create just for them. As a result, there is an increased chance that they will be more easily influenced to reciprocate any requests later down the line.

EXPERIMENT 45

The question:

Do you think that by eating your least favourite food, it is possible to like it?

YES / NO

The experiment:

In 1960 John Brehm from Duke University wanted to explore the concept of cognitive dissonance a little further.[71] In particular, he wanted to understand if a person is committed to doing something they don't enjoy over time, they will eventually come to enjoy it.

To test this study, Brehm and his team engaged a number of 8th graders from New Haven Junior High School. In the experiment, the students were given a questionnaire and on it 34 different vegetables, which they had to answer questions about. Specifically, Brehm and his team were looking for the vegetables least liked by each individual student. Armed with this knowledge and a selection of vegetables, the researchers returned to the school and told the students that they wanted to check to see if their opinion on the vegetables had changed. They then gave each child the vegetable which they scored lowest on their questionnaire (disliked the most) and asked them to see if they could eat a portion of their most disliked vegetable. If they did, they were told they would receive a prize in doing so. They were also told that their parents would be informed that they had eaten said vegetable, thus implying it would be served more at home.

Nonetheless, a few weeks later (potentially after their parents had served their least favourite vegetable to them), the researchers again gave a questionnaire for the boys to complete. Now, their initially least favourite vegetable was now their most favourite. This feedback was, of course, consistent with the dissonance theory.

Cognitive dissonance theory suggests that we all have an inner drive to hold all our attitudes and actions in harmony in order to avoid disharmony (or dissonance).

Principles of persuasion at work:

Whilst there are no principles of persuasion at work here, this experiment shows that even a physical dislike of something can be reversed and can be influenced. In this case, this was achieved by simply encouraging the children to both try and eat their least favourite vegetable more regularly.

EXPERIMENT 46

The question

If I (as part of the Road Traffic Safety Committee) visited your house and asked your permission for me to erect a DRIVE SAFELY billboard on your front lawn, are you likely to let me?

YES / NO

Would your neighbours be more open to this request if they saw you had agreed?

YES /NO

The experiment:

In 1966, Jonathan Freedman and Scott Fraser and their research team conducted an experiment to explore the 'foot-in-the-door' influence technique.[72] This is a compliance technique to influence a person to meet a greater demand by first creating a connection with the person and thus getting them to agree to a modest request.

In this experiment, the research team visited a neighbourhood and asked residents the question posed to you earlier:

"We are from the Road Traffic Safety Committee, trying to gauge people's willingness to support our 'Drive Carefully Through Our Neighbourhood Campaign and wondered if you could allow one of our team members to

place a large billboard saying DRIVE SAFELY on your front lawn".

Unsurprisingly, only 17% of all residents asked agreed to this rather large, intrusive request.

In keeping with the foot-in-the-door principle, the second experiment wanted to put this technique to the test to see if the residents who had originally declined the request could be more readily influenced. The team sent a new researcher into a new neighbourhood and this time asked the residents if they would mind placing a small inconspicuous sign saying 'Be a Safe Driver' in their front window. Nearly all of the homeowners agreed to this simple request. Three days later and the researcher returned, asking the much larger request as outlined earlier. This time the agreement to allow a large billboard to be erected on their front lawn grew to a massive 76%. The only difference between the two studies was that the researcher had originally asked them to commit to a much smaller request first. The second, much larger request psychologically encouraged the residents to act with consistency in relation to being concerned citizens. They wanted to be associated with supporting the Drive Carefully campaign.

Principles of persuasion at work:

Here, it is the commitment and consistency principles of persuasion at work. This also dovetails with the principle of consensus in that the residents would have also seen other residents committing to the campaign and acting upon the first request.

This principle of persuasion can be used outside of the behavioural psychology arena too. As an example, many life coaches and nutritionists all offer free initial consultation calls which follow the principles of the foot in the door technique. By committing to a smaller request of an initial phone call, there is a psychological shift between them being a new prospect to being a customer. The same idea can be applied in sales where even making a small sale to a client where you may make no profit as a seller again places them into the new category of a genuine customer as opposed to a prospective customer, thus changing the dynamic of the relationship and making it easier to sell a larger order to.

EXPERIMENT 47

The question:

If you saw a crumpled-up piece of paper on the street only a few feet from a bin, would you pick it up and dispose of it? (Be honest, no one is tapping into your brain and judging you either way)

YES / NO

The experiment:

In 1972, psychologist Leonard Bickman from Smith College, Massachusetts was keen to explore the relationship between belief and behaviour and how the two impacts one another.[73] Bickman and his team of researchers conducted an intriguing yet simple experiment in which they placed a crumpled up piece of litter on the street just a few feet away from the bin. With the scene set, Bickman and his team secretly filmed the pedestrians going past the bin and litter. He found that a mere 29% of those who walked past it actually put the litter in the bin.

After seeing them walk past without picking up the litter, Bickman and his team approached the pedestrians and asked them if they believed it was everyone's responsibility to pick litter up and dispose of it, or if they thought it was the responsibility of the people who are paid to do it? 94% of the people interviewed, who had previously walked past the litter without putting it in the adjacent bin, firmly believed that it was everyone's responsibility to pick up the litter and dispose of it.

Principles of persuasion at work:

Whilst there is no principle of persuasion at work here, this strange phenomenon can be attributed to the idea of doublethink, where we think one way but act another. Behavioural psychologists believe that in order to determine people's true values and beliefs, we should pay less attention to what people say and more attention to what they actually do. By taking this approach, we can apply a much more tailored principle of influence to a prospective client in a negotiation situation. Being aware of this double think is important, as it can dictate how we influence others to take action or buy certain things. Similarly, double think is not just applicable to littering but pervasive to many other parts of our lives. We say we love animals but are avid meat-eaters, or alternatively say we are concerned about the environment but don't recycle and use less energy-efficient vehicles.

EXPERIMENT 48

The question:

Do you feel more confident before you place a bet on a horse to win a race or after you've placed your bet?

BEFORE / AFTER

The experiment:

It may be difficult to answer the question above with any degree of accuracy as this is a highly situational question. Once you have placed your bet and have your betting slip in your hand, the dynamic of the question completely changes. The reason for this is because you are now tangibly invested in the bet as opposed to hypothetically thinking about it, with nothing to lose. That said, in 1968, psychologists Robert Knox and James Inkster set out to understand post-decisional dissonance (the questioning of the choice we have just made) following a commitment to bet on a horse in the natural setting of a race track.[74]

Their experiment involved 141 participants who were split into two groups. The first group of 69 participants was interviewed by the research team to allow them to understand the level of confidence they had that their horse would win before placing a $2 bet on their chosen horse. The second group, made up of 72 participants were asked the same question, but this time, they were asked after they placed their $2 bet on their chosen horse.

Based on a rating system of 7, the first group had an average confidence rating of 3.48, whilst those who had given their confidence rating after they had placed the bet had an average confidence rating of 4.81.

In both groups, the same value bet was placed, and the only variable was their mindset. This experiment has been replicated a number of times, and the results always reveal the same theme. Once a punter takes ownership of their betting slip, their mindset changes, and they see an increase in self-confidence in their actions.

This strange phenomenon is associated with social influence. People have a desire to appear consistent with the actions or behaviours they initially make and will justify these decisions if they experience external pressures questioning their choice.

Whilst a gambler may be tentative and uncertain one moment, the simple act of handing over $2 thirty seconds later means that they are much more confident in their buying decision. They become convinced they have made the correct decision, and as a result, they feel better about it. This is self-influence at its most visible.

Principles of persuasion at work:

Here we see commitment and consistency as the two overriding principles of persuasion at work. The two combined encourage people to persuade or influence themselves into making post-purchase justifications for their actions. In the field of behavioural psychology, this is referred to as 'cognitive dissonance'.

Cognitive dissonance occurs when someone experiences conflicting attitudes, behaviours or beliefs, or participates in an action that goes against any one of these. This produces a feeling of mental discomfort leading to an alteration in one of the attitudes, behaviours, or beliefs to reduce the discomfort and restore the balance.

We can influence attitudes using external persuasive stimuli such as advertising. By targeting the source, message and audience, we can effectively influence behaviours. It is possible to encourage behaviour and change through two routes. The first is focussing on delivering facts and information to the chosen audience, and the second uses more subtle clues and positive associations with what we are selling or promoting. This positive association may come in the form of beauty, fame, wealth, and positive association.

We all experience cognitive dissonance in our own lives, too, through selective exposure to information. If we are out shopping and want a nice dessert to take home from the local supermarket, we read the directions on how to prepare it, but we choose not to pay attention to any of the potentially harmful additives or excess amounts of salt and fat.

Children also exhibit displays of cognitive dissonance too. In 1962, psychologists Brehm and Cohen conducted an experiment that asked children to choose one of two toys that they had previously said they liked equally.[75] They noticed that once they had made their choice, their liking for the toy they chose went up whilst their liking for the toy they didn't choose declined.

EXPERIMENT 49

The question:

Do you think your body posture can give you more influence over people and help you negotiate more favourable deals in business?

YES / NO

The experiment:

If that question sounds like a leading one, you'd be right. No doubt you noticed this, agreed, and gave a yes as your answer. The use of body posturing can be particularly effective when we apply 'mirroring techniques', which we briefly mentioned earlier.

In 2008, researcher Stevens Maddux and his colleagues conducted a set of experiments to determine if mirroring another person can give you more influence in a negotiation.[76]

Several years prior to this, social psychologists Tanya Chartrand and John Bargh had conducted similar mirroring experiments where one of their team would tap their foot if the participant did, or fold their arms if the participant did, etc.[77] This mirroring resulted in feedback from the participant that they felt more at ease and the interaction went smoother than when another researcher purposefully did not mirror their actions in another situation.

With this in mind, Maddux wanted to see if this could be applied to the business world. For this experiment, he invited a handful of MBA students to mirror a participant whilst simultaneously negotiating a business deal, so if one of the participants leaned back on their chair, then so too would the MBA assistant and so on. He then invited a second group of MBA students to negotiate with another set of participants, but this time they were specifically told not to mirror the other person.

Maddux and his team found that an astonishing 67% of the negotiations where the participant was mirrored resulted in a deal being reached, whilst a significantly fewer 12.5% of the negotiations where mirroring was not being used reached a successful deal.

Similar to the earlier experiments conducted by Chartrand and Bargh, the participants who were being mirrored and reached a deal they were comfortable with reported to have felt more relaxed and more comfortable disclosing personal information than those participants who had not been mirrored.[78]

Principles of persuasion at work:

It is likeability which is the principle of persuasion at work here. These experiments demonstrate the power that mirroring someone else can have and how it can increase your persuasive powers and connection with someone else. When we connect with others, we will subconsciously mirror their actions and behaviours and even take on some of their attributes, grammar, and phrases.

In 2003, psychologist Rick Van Baaren found that waiters who repeated diners' orders back to them compared to saying "okay" or "I'll get that for you" found that they earned 70% more in tips. In your personal life, mirroring can also be applied verbally. Some examples may include starting a reply with the following introductions and then repeating back to them what they have suggested:

"Just so we're on the same page......."

"Just to confirm........"

"Just to reiterate......."

"So that's......."

"So your saying......."

In a similar series of negotiation studies conducted by the prominent psychologist Robert Cialdini and his research team, he invited some MBA students to carry out some negotiations. Before they began their first negotiation, they told the participant they were negotiating with, "Time is money. Let's get straight down to business." In this group, around 55% of the groups involved in the negotiation were able to come to an agreement.

Cialdini and his team invited a second set of students to repeat this experiment. This time, however, the MBA students were advised to exchange some personal information with the people they would be negotiating with before 'getting down to business'. This much more relaxed approach allowed them to identify a common goal with one another and then begin negotiations. In this group, a massive 90% of them were able to come to a successful and agreeable outcome that was typically worth 18% more to both parties.

EXPERIMENT 50

The question:

Let's imagine you have been queuing in line to be served at a supermarket for 10 minutes. Under what circumstances would you let someone go in front of you?

The experiment:

In 1978, Harvard psychologist Ellen Langar and her colleagues wanted to test if it was possible to influence people to allow them to push in front of them in a queue.[79] To put this to the test, they enrolled the help of some students to join a queue of people waiting to have their documents photocopied at a photocopying machine.

The first set of students tried to push in front of the next person in line by simply asking if they could do so, but without giving a reason to support their request. 24% of people complied and allowed them to push in front of them.

In the second set of studies, the students used the rather bizarre request of "May I use the photocopier? I have five pages I need to copy". This yielded a 60% agreement rate from people allowing them to push in front.

Finally, the third round of students posed the question – "May I use the photocopier because I'm in a rush". This resulted in a massive 94% of people agreeing to let them push in front of them

When we break both of these requests down, the reasons are extremely weak. All of the people in the queue want to make a copy, so the first reason has little credibility. Similarly, most people are in a rush and would prefer not to be waiting in a photocopier queue; so again, this second reason has little credibility either. However, despite this, both requests had been granted simply by inserting the word 'because' into the sentence. This gave credibility and reason for wanting to jump the queue despite the absurdness of the reason itself.

Principles of persuasion at work:

Whilst there are no principles of persuasion at work here, exploiting peoples' Fixed Behaviour Response Patterns (FRPs) did allow the students to move in front of the next person in the queue. Fixed response patterns occur in response to a certain sign or stimulus – in this case, the word 'because'. The word 'because' was then followed by a good enough reason or justification despite its lack of credibility.

When the stakes are low (in this case, simply photocopying something), people are more likely to make mental shortcuts when they hear the word 'because' and associate it with a justification and allow permission to the person making the request. However, when the stakes are high, the request is taken much more seriously, and any responses will be much more considered and measured. For example: "Can I have 50% off the price of this TV because I spent my money on my golf membership" will not result in activating in the fixed response pattern.

We can apply this principle both at work and in our private lives when making requests to people by justifying our request, using the word 'because'. In this way, we stand a much greater chance of persuading someone to agree with our request compared to if the stakes were low. However, if we are in a position of authority, using the phrase 'because someone else said so' can actually dilute this position of authority and the request is less likely to be granted. It is far better to give a more tangible reason to support your request.

It is also worth encouraging any clients who are happy with your products or services to give you testimonials for your business and use the word 'because' in their feedback. This gives a level of credibility, authenticity, and weight to their review as it increases the specificity. It also allows others to pinpoint what points the reviewer found particularly inspiring or beneficial and means they will be more likely to be persuaded to buy your products and services rather than if the testimonial simply gave a star rating and a generic review such as "Duncan was brilliant!"

EXPERIMENT 51

The question:

This question requires you to get a few items; 3 matchboxes and a small handful of coins.

Follow the steps in order:

1. Ensure the matchboxes are the same. (If you can't do this now, just visualize it and make your guess at the end. If you are intrigued about the answer and want it confirming, try it out when you get the chance). Once you have the three matchboxes, fill one of them with coins and then stack that one on top of the other two as though they're a pile of books.
2. The next step is to pick all three matchboxes up using your dominant hand gripping the box closest to the table with your thumb and forefinger, and lifting all three matchboxes 1 inch off the table. Once you've done that, replace them all on the table.
3. You are now going to lift the top match box off the top other three by about an inch, using the same thumb and forefinger grip.

Do you think the matchbox felt lighter, heavier, or as you expect it to?

For those of you who have done this, a wry smile should have come over your face as the top matchbox filled with coins should now feel a lot heavier than you had imagined.

The reason this unusual illusion works is due to a principle called 'perceptual contrast'. In reality, the box of matches with the coins inside should feel as you expect them to. However, because you have lifted all three identical-looking matchboxes together, your mind makes the assumption that because they all look the same, they should all weigh the same. Your mind assumes that the final matchbox will weigh a third of the combined weight instead of the full weight.

The experiment:

To support the experiment above, psychologists Zakary Tomala and Richard Petty wanted to explore the principle of 'perceptual contrast' further and understand if it could be applied in business and to our personal lives to influence others.[80] Perceptual contrast is the idea that our perception of something is affected by the context in which it is placed. Thus if we see two things in sequence that are different from one another, we will tend to see the second one as more different from the first than it actually is. To put this principle to the test, Tomala and Petty devised an experiment to see if it could be used to influence how people think.

Rather than using tangible objects, specifically, they wanted to see if the amount of information people think they have about something can be influenced by the amount of information they learn about something else.

To start with, Tomala, Petty, and their team of researchers invited some participants to read a persuasive message about a fictitious department store called 'Browns'. This was their 'target message', and throughout the experiment, this message would not change.

They also encouraged these same participants to read a 'prior message' before they read the target message. This 'prior message' was of an equally persuasive tone to the target message and was related to another department store, called 'Smiths'.

Throughout the experiment, when the prior message (Smiths) was altered so that it contained more information than the target message and read before the target message, the target message (Browns) was found to be less persuasive and produced less favourable attitudes towards it.

The opposite occurred when the prior message contained very little information compared to the target message. In this instance, the participants felt that they were more knowledgeable about the target message (Browns) after learning relatively little from the 'prior message' (Smiths). They also found the target message to be more persuasive, and the participants had an even more favourable attitude towards Browns.

Similar to the matchbox experiment, this example emphasizes the strength of perceptual contrast and its ability to influence our perception of something if it is used in the correct context. This is especially true when it is not perceived by itself, but in comparison to something else, in this case, a rival department store.

The study became even more intriguing when the researchers delivered a prior message completely unrelated to the target message about the department store. In this instance, the preceding message focussed on the attributes of a Mini Cooper car.

Surprisingly, the results were exactly the same as the first study, regardless of the length of the preceding message. In this case, a short prior message (related to the car) produced much more favourable results about the target message (related to the department store). This emphasizes that the prior message doesn't even have to be relevant to the target message to also be persuasive about it.

Principles of persuasion at work:

Whilst there are no principles of persuasion at play here, the principle of 'perceptual contrast' can be a powerful technique to influence others to buy your product or service if used in the correct context.

Outside of the sphere of behavioural psychology, perceptual contrast could also be applied to whisky (or alcohol). If I were to give you a suggestion to the price of a five-year-old bottle of whisky, this would affect your perception as to what you'd pay for that same bottle of whisky that had been aged for fifteen years. While the price of the first bottle of whiskey I gave you is not related to the second, your mind is keen to find coherence between the two and uses the first value to create a value of the second.

It's rare to have the resources at your disposal to evaluate two things side-by-side, so the best you can do is relate one value to the other.

In the sales arena, if you are confident that your product or service is the best fit for the client, but there may be another item that you want to steer them away from, you could use the perceptual contrast principle here. You could start by briefly mentioning your competitor's product in your 'prior message' and then deliver a more substantive persuasive message about your product in your 'target message'. This same technique can also be applied when describing alternative products in your portfolio. The purpose of this would be to ensure customer retention for both your products and maybe even your membership services. This is also the most cost-effective and time-efficient way to promote new initiatives, products, and services to current or new customers and clients by again using the same perceptual contrast principle.

Didn't have some matchboxes?

For those of you who did not get the chance to take part in the matchbox experiment, you could try the following to offer another more physical representation of the perceptual contrast principle, now it's been explained in more detail.

Get yourself three buckets or bowls of water. Fill the first one with hot (but not boiling) water, the second with cold water, and finally, fill the third with warm water. Now plunge your right hand into the bucket of cold water and your left hand into the bucket of hot water. Leave them there for about 20 seconds. Now remove both of your hands together and plunge them into the bucket filled with warm water at the same time.

You'll notice that your right hand will perceive this water as hot, and your left hand will perceive this water as cold. Again this is a beautiful representation of the perceptual contrast principle, which reiterates that the item, service, product, or in this instance, the temperature of our hands are not perceived as one but in contrast to the other.

EXPERIMENT 52

The question:

If children are able to see themselves in a mirror behind a jar of sweets, do you think they are more or less likely to take more than they had previously been allowed?

MORE / LESS

The experiment:

In 1979, social psychologist Arthur Beaman and his team of researchers wanted to explore the relationship between self-awareness and transgressive behaviour.[81] (Transgressive behaviour is defined as exceeding a limit or boundary, especially of social acceptability). In the first experiment of two, Beaman and his team of researchers took over local houses (with permission) on the night of Halloween, and for every trick or treater who came to the door (Three hundred and sixty-three of them), they chose the treat option and told children they could take one sweet only.

They then told them they had to go and continue with their work, thus leaving them and the bowl of sweets unaccompanied. The researchers were, in fact, recording how many children took more than the one sweet allowed. With the children thinking that no one was watching, the researchers found that 33.7% of the children opted to take more 'treats' than they were allowed.

In the second experiment, the researchers positioned a mirror behind the bowl of sweets so the children could see their own reflections. Again a similar number of children were involved (349), but this time when the researchers left the room and left the children alone with the bowl of sweets and their own face looking back at them in the reflection of the mirror; they found that the rate of theft declined, with just 8.9% of children taking more than the permitted sweet.

In 2000, researcher Carl Kallgren wanted to explore the findings from these experiments further to see if the relationship between self-awareness and transgressive behaviour was equally applicable to adults as it was to children.[82] In this experiment, Kallgren invited a series of adult participants into his lab, explaining to them that he and his team were conducting an experiment that would be monitoring their heart rates. He split the participants into two groups and ensured that the first group saw themselves on a CCTV recording, similar to the children in Beaman's experiment seeing themselves in a mirror. The other group did not see themselves on CCTV but instead simply watched a screen displaying geometric shapes.

For the experiment, Kallgren and his team asked the participants to smear a gel-like substance on their hands to assist with the monitoring of their heart rates. At the end of both fictitious experiments, all participants were given a paper hand towel before leaving the lab and heading downstairs. With no rubbish bin available, Kallgren and his team were keen to see how many of the participants would throw their paper towels on the floor in the stairwell, thinking that no one was watching. In fact, Kallgren and his team were watching. They found that 46% of the participants who had not seen themselves on CCTV in the fictitious experiment littered their paper towels in the stairwell, whilst a more respectable 24% of those who had seen themselves on CCTV threw their paper towels on the floor when they believed no one was watching.

Principles of persuasion at work:

Whilst there are no principles of persuasion at work here, these experiments demonstrate how influential something can be when we see a reflection or image of ourselves and how it can influence us to act and think differently.

Self-influence can act as a huge motivator. Whilst a large portion of this book focuses on influencing others to achieve the desired result, self-influence is an equally potent technique to master. Self-influence can give you the inner drive to succeed at something and motivate yourself into achieving your goals without needing the accountability of a personal trainer or coach who will never wholly understand your drivers and needs anyway. If you find something inside of you that unsettles you, this can be an even more powerful form of self-influence than being unsettled by something outside of you. One technique to achieve this if you want to find that inner drive to help you lose weight, as an example, is to look at your naked body in a full-length mirror. As many of us are critical of our own looks, this may persuade us to make a change. Again, if we want to lose weight, another tried and tested self-influence technique is to install a mirror in your fridge. When reaching for extra food, the mirror makes you more self-conscious, more self-aware, and easier to self-influence, making you more likely to put that snickers bar back and close the door.

EXPERIMENT 53

The question:

The principles of persuasion, when combined with the OCEAN model, can increase your persuasion and influence skills massively. Do you think that these same techniques could help people of different nationalities achieve the same success?

YES / NO

The experiment:

Having spent a number of years living in Japan and travelling to over 25 countries, giving talks, consulting, and delivering my masterclasses to many different nationalities and cultures, I, of course, notice many cultural differences in the business world. To support these observations, I found some wonderful experiments that have been conducted that highlight how different cultures respond and use different influence and persuasion techniques.

In 2007, behavioural psychologists Petia Petrova, Robert Cialdini, and an accompanying research team set out to explore the cross-cultural consistencies and inconsistencies between Americans and Asians.[83] In their collaborative experiment, they sent out several emails with surveys to be completed to both American and Asian students.

Two months after this first email was sent, a second survey was emailed. The recipients were informed that although it would take twice as long as the first survey to complete, it is related to the first one, so it is essential it is completed.

In the first request, the American students complied with the request less than the Asian demographic. However, in the second request, Petrova and her team found that of those who did comply with the first request, it was the Americans who were more likely to respond to the second request. In percentage terms, 22% of Americans completed the second survey if they completed the first, whilst 10% of Asians completed the second survey if they had completed the first.

This evidence demonstrates that by complying with the first request (to complete the survey), the Americans were more likely to comply with the second request (complete the survey) than the Asians. As a result, the Americans were more influenced by their prior (or historical) agreement to complete the first task. A follow-up study found that whilst the Asian demographic was not influenced in the same way as the Americans, Asian cultures would have been more influenced if it was communicated that their peers had also completed the first survey.

Other behavioural psychology studies over time support a similar view between cultures. American's, Western Europeans and Canadians are more widely regarded to be individualists.[84] This means that they focus more on their individual goals and the rights and behaviours of the individual person. Asians, Eastern Europeans, South American's and Africans tend to be more collectivists. This means that they focus more on group goals and interpersonal relationships and consider others when deciding what is best for the collective group.

Principles of persuasion at work:

The principle of persuasion at work in this example is that of commitment and consistency. In the aforementioned regions, which focus more on individualism, their future actions and behaviours are more heavily influenced when they are reminded of their past actions or behaviours to maintain a level of consistency. Conversely, those countries that are more focused on collectivism place a much greater weight on what other people have done before to influence their own actions and behaviours.

When influencing a person from an individualistic country such as America or the UK, it's important to use a language that focuses on the person as an individual and their personal actions to unlock their levels of compliance. Placing it into context, if you were making a request to a person from an individualistic country, you might say something like this:

"I really appreciate what you have done......can you also do this."

Here the focus is on personal consistency.

Conversely, countries such as China, Brazil or Poland, which focus more on the actions of their peer group, would require a different approach:

"I really appreciate what you and the rest of your colleagues have done.....can you also do this".

Here this focus is more on social proof, therefore they are more likely to be persuaded into making a certain decision by highlighting what their peer group have previously done.

EXPERIMENT 54

The question:

Do you find it easy to leave an answerphone message, and if not, why not?

YES / NO + REASON

The experiment:

In 2006, Yuri Miyamoto and Norbert Schwarz turned their psychologist brains towards the analysis of collectivism and individualism.[85] They wanted to understand if belonging to either one of these groups could affect their behaviour when it comes to leaving an answerphone message.

With communication driven more through relational content for people from collectivist countries and more informational content for people from individualistic countries, cultures that belong to these two groups provide interesting variations when it comes to leaving answerphone messages. In the study, Miyamoto and Schwarz evaluated the answerphone-leaving habits of Japanese and American participants.

After analysing hundreds of participants and phone calls, they found that the Japanese took a longer period of time to leave a message than their American counterparts. They surmised that this was due to their increased levels of concern with how the recipient would receive this message. Americans, on the other hand, were more driven by conveying a message and ensuring the recipients received the facts and the information with less regard for the type of reception it would get from them.

In Miyamoto and Schwarz's studies, they found that Americans left a message half the time whilst the Japanese didn't even leave a message at all 85% of the time.

As a collectivist nation, there are ingrained cultural differences that result in the Japanese behaving like this compared to a more individualist nation like America. One of the main reasons they don't leave a voice message is in order to preserve their social and business relationships.[86]

From Miyamoto and Schwarz's study, when the Japanese were asked what they disliked most about leaving an answerphone message, they cited more relational reasons associated with their cultural collectivism, such as "It is hard to sound personal on the answering machine". American's on the other hand, cited more informational reasons in keeping with their culture of individualism, suggesting that "Sometimes people don't check it".

From my time in Japan, another major cultural difference comes in the form of the level of response that is given to the speaker. When people from individualist cultures speak to one another, an intermittent acknowledgement of what is being said is culturally acceptable by saying 'yes' 'uh-huh' or a simple nodding of the head.[87]

However, in Japan, a constant 'hai' (meaning yes) is standard communication practice to demonstrate to the other person that you are still actively involved and engaged in the conversation. This response to the speaker is significantly more frequent and is noticeable when you visit the country or watch any programme that shares an insight into their culture on TV.

With an answerphone message, however, cultures similar to Japan do not receive this feedback, and as a result, Miyamoto and Schwarz suggest that for many Japanese, leaving an answerphone message is as though they are not speaking to anyone. They described the experience as "hard to speak when there are no responses".

Principles of persuasion at work:

Whilst there are no principles of persuasion at work here, cultural considerations should be taken into account when engaging with different cultures. It is important to consider whether the company or person is from a culture that embraces either a collectivist or individualist approach to communication and relationships. This will allow you to finesse the way that you communicate and ensure you can yield the best results out of the conversation or engagement. Similarly, by being sensitive to their cultural norms, you will find you'll be able to influence people from other cultures more successfully than your peers.

EXPERIMENT 55

The question:

Imagine you have just checked into a hotel after a long day. You have just finished showering and see one of the following five signs.

Which of the following would be more likely to encourage you more to reuse your towel?

A. Help The Hotel Save Energy
B. Help Save The Planet
C. Partner With Us To Help Save The Planet
D. Help Save Resources For Future Generations
E. Please Join Your Fellow Guests In Helping Save The Planet. 75% of guests participate in our Resource Savings Program by using their towel more than once

A / B / C / D / E

The experiment:

Prominent psychologist Robert Cialdini and his team wanted to investigate if changing the wording on hotel signs that requested guests to re-use their towels could influence more of them to participate in the request. In order to undertake this test, Cialdini and his team of researchers created five signs, with the wording detailed the same as above.[88]

In order to find out which one of the signs would influence the most people to reuse their towels, they displayed the five signs across multiple hotel rooms and asked the hotel staff to monitor which signs contributed the most to towel re-usage.

They found that in comparison to the hotel rooms where no signs were being displayed, signs A-D encouraged 16% more guests to use their towels.

Sign E had an even greater impact, and a huge 44% of guests reused their towels.

Cialdini and his team believed they could go one better, and they tweaked the wording on the final sign even more and devised the following:

"Please join your fellow guests in helping save the planet. 75% of guests staying in this room use their towels more than once".

This is now encouraged a massive 49% of guests to reuse their towels compared to the 16% with the more generic signs A-D.

Principles of persuasion at work:

The aforementioned experiment is one of the most widely cited experiments relating to the power of social proof or consensus. Both are seen as powerful principles of persuasion. There are two underpinning psychological notions at work here. The first plays on the idea that if other people believe in something, then it is more than likely to be true.

The second notion is based on the idea that our brain uses clues and cues or mental shortcuts to judge the value and validity of something. In the experiment above, it demonstrates that you don't even have to hear or see something, and it can just be the idea that can persuade someone into doing something.

Another commonly used phrase to describe the principle of social proof is the 'wisdom of crowds'. In similarity to dogs – if one dog starts barking, another will start barking too. Not knowing why the first dog started in the first place, very soon, all the other dogs that can hear will join in, without any of them knowing why the first dog started.

The experiment conducted by Cialdini and his team emphasises that you don't need incentives to make big changes or to influence others; you can simply use the science and psychology behind the persuasive techniques.

In conclusion, if you are looking to influence others, it is more powerful to point to what other people are doing or saying than trying to influence the person yourself. This technique is amplified even further if the people you point others to are similar to them. This similarity could come in the form of their attitude, behaviour, demographic, geographic location or even that they are their friends.

EXPERIMENT 56

The question:

This question starts with a little experiment you can try yourself. Find yourself an elastic band and hook it around your wrist. Go on. This is important to visualise one of the most powerful experiments in this book. If you have done that, now pull this back and let the band flick back against the underside of your wrist. This is the equivalent pain you would receive if someone administered a 10-15v electric shock.

Based on the pain you felt there if you were to attach that same rubber band on someone else, how many equivalent volts of pain would you be happy to administer to them if they failed to answer your test questions correctly?

20 volts / 100 volts / 450 volts?

The experiment:

In 1963, psychologist Stanley Milgram conducted an experiment that focussed on authority as the principle of persuasion.[89] History is littered with people being influenced to behave against their better judgement and out of nature simply because an authority figure is telling them to do so. They have been made to act in heinous and deviant ways that are so out of character with their personality they are left questioning their actions. To understand why people commit such atrocious acts, he invited a series of participants to his lab.

Working in teams of two, one would be designated the role of the teacher, and the other the role of student. Even at this early stage in the experiment, Milgram was setting the stage. In fact, there was only one participant in this experiment. The other person was part of Milgram's research team, who was going to play the role of the student. The third member of this psychological experiment was a scientist (another member of the research team) whose role it was to act like a scientist. A long white lab coat added to his credentials and helped give him the position of authority required for this.

To ensure that the genuine participant played the role of the teacher, the scientist allowed them to choose one of two pieces of paper which 'supposedly' had one saying teacher and the other saying student, but in fact, they both had the word 'teacher' on them, so no matter which they chose it would say the word teacher. The research assistant who was playing the role of the student simply miscalled his word as 'student'.

Once the scientist, participant and researcher (playing the role of the student) were all in the same room, the scientist then told the student that he would be asked a series of memory questions by the teacher. These would involve remembering pairs of words, and then the teacher would offer them a number of multiple choices from which they should choose.

If the answer given was incorrect, the teacher would administer an electric shock. To demonstrate, the teacher (genuine participant) and student (stooge) were taken to an adjacent room. The teacher was then connected to a generator which supposedly administered a series of electric shocks ranging from 15 volts all the way up to a lethal 450 volts. To put it in perspective, a domestic UK electricity supply is 240 volts. The teacher then experienced the pain that a 15-volt current causes when the generator was switched on. (The pain is similar to the elastic band test used in the mini-experiment at the start of this experiment).

The student then supposedly had both his wrists connected to the generator, and the scientist ushered the teacher into the adjacent room where the generator and switches to control the number of volts that could be administered were. After the student (stooge) was on his own, he was able to slip out of the connectors and attach the same connectors to a recording device. The device had pre-recorded screams and requests to stop the experiment, which were piped into the teacher's electric shock administration room and was activated when a shock was administered.

After allowing time for the student to 'supposedly' memorise the word pairs, the test began. The scientist, who had reinforced his position of authority by conducting proceedings, then gave the teacher a series of questions and told them they should increase the voltage each time the student gets a question wrong.

The purpose of this test is now, hopefully, apparent. Milgram and his team wanted to see if the teachers (genuine participants) will call a stop to the experiment when they hear the cries of help from the student they are electrocuting or will they continue, simply because a person in a position of authority is telling them to continue? Milgram and his team were intrigued to see if people would obey authority to the point where they would go as far as administering potentially lethal shocks.

Each time the teacher read out a question, the automated response would kick in, and it would reply with an incorrect answer. As per the rules of the experiment, the teacher then had to administer the electric shock in response to this wrong answer. Once they had administered the shock, the teacher then had to increase the voltage by 15 volts for the next set of questions. Each time, the replies to the questions were incorrect, and each time the teacher heard cries of help and requests for them to stop. If there was no reply to the question within 4 to 5 seconds, the teacher was instructed to shock the student regardless.

Milgram and his team believed that most people would abandon the experiment after just a few incremental rises in the level of voltage being administered to the student. Statistically, they thought that only 1% of all participants would continue till the end of the experiment. They were wrong.

In fact, over 50% of teachers (genuine participants) went all the way up to shocking the participant with a lethal 450 volts even when they heard no cries for help (as though the participant and passed out or the shocks had killed them). Even when they hesitated about the ethics of the test and questioned the health condition of the student, the scientist still asked them to complete the test. Obeying his authority, they pressed on despite these concerns.

Principles of persuasion at work:

Due to the nature of this test, a replication of this experiment is banned in most countries now, yet only one demonstration is really needed to highlight the power of authority as a principle of persuasion.

People are more readily influenced by others who they perceive as knowledgeable, credible experts. In this instance, something as simple as a scientist wearing a white lab coat was sufficient to convey these traits of authority. People allow themselves to be guided by people in positions of authority as it gives them a sense that their actions or behaviour is acceptable.

As mentioned earlier in this book, rather than telling others about your position of authority, it is far more powerful for people to come to their own conclusions, draw their own inferences or be informed by others.

EXPERIMENT 57

The question:

Read this article: http://news.bbc.co.uk/1/hi/uk/4268260.stm

Alternatively, open the photo app on your phone and hold it over this QR code. It will take you to the site, and have a read:

The question is this: Forgetting that this is a book predominantly focussed on influence for a second, would you say that the study is credible or not? Do you also believe that by analysing brain activity, one can develop a mathematical formula that could detect lies from the truth with 99% accuracy?

YES / NO

The experiment:

In 2008, researchers David P. McCabe and Alan D. Castel conducted an experiment to understand whether seeing brain images next to an article affects our judgements of scientific reasoning.[90] They showed participants in their experiment the article above and claimed that brain scans could be used as lie detectors. (In summary, that article suggests that if you are placed in an MRI scanner and asked to think of a lie, the part of the brain associated with complex thinking, your frontal lobe, becomes very active. This suggests that you are going to make up a lie).

However, there was a flaw in this experiment. Your frontal lobe may not become active because you are speaking a lie, but more because you are creatively imagining a lie. The only way to really conduct this test would be to use criminals and quiz them on their lies (but then we must know they are lies), so it all gets a little suspect.

Principles of persuasion at work:

Despite the flaws in this experiment, it does show how powerful authority is as a principle of persuasion. If we read an article that has an image of an MRI scan of a brain next to it, we automatically assume it is more credible and has greater tendencies to be influenced by it. In today's news, we are swamped by 'fake news' with the term 'clickbait' becoming ever more widely used within the reporting industry. Scientific articles, images of scans of the brain or photographs of authority figures placed at the top of an article (sometimes out of context) influence us to believe the content reported or the facts contained therein.

EXPERIMENT 58

The question:

"How are you today?" Or "How are you feeling today?" have become a somewhat ubiquitous form of saying hello, but do you think you would be more likely to invite a stranger (with the appropriate credentials) into your house if they prefaced any subsequent question with one of these two enquiry questions about your wellbeing?

YES / NO / MAYBE

The experiment:

In 1990, psychologist Daniel Howard from the Southern Methodist University, Cox School of Business, wanted to examine if people were more likely to agree to something if they had something positive said to them before they were given a choice to agree or disagree with something.[91] In the experiment, his researchers, cold-called some random members of the public and asked if a representative from the Hunger Relief Committee could arrange a visit to sell them some biscuits for charity. Howard briefed half of the researchers to begin the call, with the question "How are you this evening?" and the others to ask no introductory question.

The researchers would then ask if arranging a visit was possible. They found that by eliciting an initial positive response from half of the people they cold-called, that 32% accepted their offer whilst those who were not asked a question, and therefore had had no positive emotion elicited, a mere 18% agreed to the representative coming over. This simple experiment confirmed that whilst not everyone could be influenced by eliciting a positive response from them before making their request, it did make a difference.

Principles of persuasion at work:

Likeability is the principle of persuasion used here, however, this specific technique is more commonly known as the "Foot in the door" technique or 'yes ladder'.

The theory behind a yes ladder is that that when a prospective client becomes used to saying yes to your smaller requests, this will have put them in such a positive state of mind that agreeing to the deal is the next, most natural answer. Yes, ladders set a perfect precedence for compliance as people will continue to build on their positive agreement.

An example of this may be:

Question 1: Tom, have you considered any extra sales training since starting your job? (Those that answer no, you're not likely to be targeting)

Prospect: Yes

Question 2: So you'd be interested in increasing your influence and persuasion skills then?

Prospect: Oh yes!

Question 3: Great! We've got a brilliant new influence coach coming in next week to hold some sessions which will definitely benefit you. Is this of interest?

Prospect: OH YES!

Me: Fantastic! The courses on offer include an interactive workshop, and I am going to deliver a really fun keynote presentation too!

After the prospect has said yes to you two or three times in a row, it makes it much more psychologically difficult for them to decline finding out more information. If the conversation was held over the phone, it makes it difficult for them to excuse themselves too.

Positive language and its positioning within a sentence can also be hugely influential in adverts too.

In 1999, psychologist Alexander Rothman and his team of researchers demonstrated this in an experiment where they encouraged participants to read one of two pamphlets about mouthwash.[92]

The first pamphlet read: "Mouthwash helps fight plaque", which focussed more on a positive style of language. The second pamphlet had a more negative tone: "Failing to use mouthwash leads to plaque build-up". Both pamphlets essentially said the same thing, but 67% of the participants who read the positive pamphlet ordered a free sample of the mouthwash compared to just 47% of the participants who read the negative one.

EXPERIMENT 59

The question:

Imagine there are two people. The first regards himself as an extremely caring person and the other less so. There is a man slumped in a doorway, clearly in agony and requiring assistance. The first man who regards himself as extremely caring is in a rush for an appointment when he sees the ailing man. The second man, who is less caring, also sees the man slumped in the doorway, but he has plenty of time to get to his appointment.

Of the two men who see the struggling man, which one is most likely to help?

THE CARING MAN IN A RUSH / THE LESS CONSIDERATE MAN WITH PLENTY OF TIME

The experiment:

In 1973, psychologists John Darley and Daniel Baston from Princeton University wanted to examine whether contextual factors had an effect on behaviour and influence.[93]

They began by questioning forty trainee priests about their motivation to join the priesthood. They wanted to ascertain whether their motivation was more focused on helping others or securing their own passage to heaven. After completing the questionnaires, they were instructed to give a five-minute talk on a chosen subject. They would be giving their talk elsewhere in the building and were issued with a map and directions on how to get there.

The trainee priests were acting as the participants in this experiment and were split into six groups. One third was told that they were running late for their presentation and really needed to be there a few minutes ago. This group was classed as the 'High hurry group'.

The second third was told that the assistant is ready and waiting and they should make their way over as soon as possible. This group was defined as the 'intermediate hurry group'.

The final third was told that the assistant would be ready in a few minutes and to make their way over there, but once they arrive, they may have to wait, and if they do, it wouldn't be for a long time. This group was classed as the 'low hurry group'.

These three groups were then subdivided into two further groups based on the topics that they would be presenting. Half would be talking about the Good Samaritan (a biblical story about a Samaritan who helps a man who had recently been robbed). The other half was to give a presentation on 'jobs best suited to graduates'.

Darley and Boston then arranged for a research assistant to play the role of someone distressed. The man played a similar role to the one described in the original question – bent over, groaning and coughing and clearly in need of some assistance.

Of all of the 40 trainee priests, only 16 stopped to help the man. This was equivalent to 40%. Of these 16 priests, 63% from the low hurry group stopped to assist, 45% of the intermediate hurry group stopped, whilst a mere 10% of the high hurry group stopped. Of all of these, it made no additional difference whether the student priests were about to give a presentation about the Good Samaritan or about jobs most suitable for graduates.

Principles of persuasion at work:

Whilst there are no principles of persuasion at work here, this eye-opening experiment suggests that it was the situation of the students being late that determined their behaviour and responses to the man in stress. It also highlights that their personality had little impact on the situation, and their involvement with the priesthood or upcoming reading of the Good Samaritan played a minimal role in their decision making. Many of the priests were so focused on getting to their presentation that they were unable to fully process the other situation. Above all, these results emphasise that it's the context and situation of an event that plays an equally important role in influencing others. This experiment demonstrates how it can even trump their personality.

In another example, described in 'The Person and the Situation: Perspectives of Social Psychology', and conducted by the renowned psychologist, Lee Ross, he invited 36 students to participate in a quiz. Half of the participants were assigned the role of questioner, whilst the other half were contestants.[94]

Ross and his team then allocated the questioners 15 minutes to think of as many tricky questions about a particular topic as they could. He then gave the contestants 15 minutes to answer these questions. At the end of the experiment, Ross and his team asked both the questioners and contestants to rate each other's general knowledge.

They found that the contestants rated the questioners much higher than the questioners rated the contestants. In a similar vein to Darley and Boston's earlier experiment, the participants in this experiment incorrectly attributed the other person's general knowledge ability to their personality rather than the context of the situation.

One of the main takeaways from all of these experiments is the need for attention from any prospective clients you may have. If you haven't managed to cultivate their attention, then it should be of utmost importance before proceeding to engage in any form of persuasion or negotiation to ensure any level of success.[95]

Our continued use of social media has meant that for many people, their attention spans have got considerably shorter than, say, ten years ago. As a result, as members of your target audience flit from one piece of media to another or one piece of information to the next, capturing their attention is becoming increasingly important. (We will discuss attention hooks and capturing attention later). In fact, research from a UK attention technology company, Lumen Research, has found that only 4% of digital ads get more than 1 second of attention whilst only 1 out of 5 ads get looked at, at all.

EXPERIMENT 60

The question:

Think about your weekly visit to your supermarket. One UK supermarket, Sainsbury's, has on average 30,000 items in their product range.

Over the course of the year, how many of these different items do you buy at one point or another?

1. Less than but no more than 200 different items
2. Less than but no more than 500 different items
3. Less than but no more than 1,000 different items
4. Less than but no more than 5,000 different items
5. Less than but no more than 10,000 different items
6. Less than but no more than 20,000 different items

The experiment:

The answer to the question 'A' and, more specifically, is 150. Incredible to think, really, but out of all the different products we could buy, we limit ourselves to just 0.5% of the range. Why? More often than not, it's simply habitual.

In 2002, psychologists Wendy Wood, Jeffrey Quinn and Deborah

Kashy from the University of Southern California conducted an experiment to understand how habits influence our thoughts, emotions and actions.[96] They believed that our actions and behaviours are half habitual and half behaviour based.

In their experiment, they recruited 27 undergraduates and issued them all with watches that buzzed at specific intervals throughout the day. The students were to stop what they were doing and record their activity at the time, whether they were eating, washing, socialising or exercising. They found that approximately 45% of everyday behaviours tended to be repeated in the same location almost every day. Not only that but the same decisions were also being made at the same time and place almost every single day. The participant's diary entries also showed that when they were performing habitual activities such as cleaning their teeth or washing, they were more likely to think about behaviours unrelated to that behaviour. When the environment changed, however, or they performed non-habitual actions, their thoughts tended to correspond more closely to their behaviours and suggested that these thought processes guide their actions.

Wood, Quinn and Kashy also found that for every changing life event that resulted in a different environment, this would destabilise their habitual behaviour. These life changes could include a new job, promotion, new partner, new car or new house.

Psychologists Laura Weston and Richard Shotton attempted to quantify the importance of these moments by conducting their own experiment.[97] They surveyed 2,370 nationally representative customers with two questions:

1. Which life events had they recently undergone?

2. Had they changed brands in a series of ten categories, including broadband providers, opticians, coffee shops etc.?

Their insightful study found that of these 60 variables (life events and ten potential brand changes), 8% of them had switched brands in one of the ten selected categories when they hadn't undergone a recent, major life event. This rose to 21% among those who had undergone a recent major life event.

Principles of persuasion at work:

Habits are behaviour patterns that dominate the neural pathways of our brain. They are the automatic actions we perform without giving much thought. As a result, it can sometimes be difficult to influence change in someone who is habitually hard-wired to a particular act or pattern of behaviour. That said, if we are able to communicate our message of persuasion before these habits solidify, then they can become more malleable. In the workplace, if someone is regularly late for work or late back from their lunch break, allowing this habit to set in can make it more difficult to influence the change of their habits than if they are persuaded against this tardiness in the first place.

Outside of the workplace, this same awareness should be applied to people who pay their utility or tax bills late. If they get used to having reminder letters sent, then this becomes a habit.

For those whose habitual behaviours and actions are already entrenched, drawing attention to these can sometimes jolt them out of it. If the persuasive message is communicated at the right time and place when their automatic or habitual behaviour is happening, this can awaken their conscious state and increase their awareness of their compulsive actions.

And so, we come full circle to the question posed at the start of this experiment. Sainsbury's acknowledged that its' customers had become habitual purchasers of the same 150 or so items and wanted to encourage them to expand the range of products they bought. They partnered with Jamie Oliver (a popular TV chef on British television screens) to create recipe cards that detailed more adventurous foods that many of their shoppers hadn't bought before. They accompanied recipe cards with a persuasive advertising message - 'Try something new today' and supported it with strong in-store point-of-sale. This campaign was aimed to persuade their customer's to expand upon the range of groceries they habitually bought. This commitment to creating a change in their customer's habits was strengthened even further by training all 150,000 members of staff.[98]

As a result of this campaign, Sainsbury's achieved a sales-led profit recovery and generated an extra £2.5 billion in revenue simply by asking their customers to 'Try Something New Today'. In turn, this same campaign encouraged each shopper to spend an extra £1.14 every time they shopped.

Whilst this example shows how you could target customer's entrenched habits at the location where these habitual behaviours take place, it is also possible to target the time when these habits are activated too.

We regularly showcase to the world, via social media, when we have just got engaged, married, moved house, bought a puppy, got promoted or become a parent or grandparent. As well as sharing our good news online, we make public announcements on the same platforms about our distaste for bad customer service, being over billed or having to wait a long time in a queue or other examples. By making these announcements, it also telegraphs that our habits are potentially open to being changed. With people being three times more likely to change their habits whilst undergoing a life event, this gives the negotiator, influencer or persuader extra leverage when it comes to prying them away from their old habits, brands, shops or services they have been habitually faithful to.

EXPERIMENT 61

The question:

Do you think you are more or less likely to read an advert if you are in a happy, relaxed mood?

YES / NO

The experiment:

In 2007, psychologist Fred Bonner from the University of Amsterdam and his team were keen to find out if the advertisements people are exposed to are more or less likely to be read dependent on their mood.[99] Whilst this theory is generally agreed upon in the world of behavioural psychology, Bonner and his team wanted to test this theory outside of laboratory conditions which could potentially distort their mood. In this study, he created a real-life field study that simulated a more naturalistic context.

Bonner and his team showed 1287 participants various newspapers and then asked them questions about the ads they had seen. They then split their results by the reader's moods. Bonner and his team found that those in a relaxed mood noticed 56% of the ads, whilst those in a stressed mood noticed just 36% of the ads.

Bonner and his team then drilled down even further to find even more intriguing insights. In a questionnaire that asked the participants to rate the quality of their day, those who strongly agreed that their day had gone really well noticed 46% of the ads, whilst those who said they had had an awful day saw just 26% of the ads.

This evidence clearly demonstrates that those people in a good mood see much more advertising and are, therefore, more receptive to being influenced. One reason for this is that when you are in a better mood, you are generally calmer and therefore being focussed on the present moment is much easier. In contrast, if you are more stressed, you may be worried or anxious about what may happen in the future or has happened in your past. These worries prevent you from being in the present moment. In doing so, it reduces your ability to retain and then recall the messages you have seen.

Principles of persuasion at work:

Whilst this experiment does not demonstrate any clear principle of persuasion, it is clear that people can both absorb and recall ads more when they are relaxed or in a good mood. Being stressed or worried inhibits the effectiveness of the persuasive nature of ads. It is, therefore, important to target your persuasive messages to your target audience at the correct time. Evidence shows that we are the most relaxed on Sunday - traditionally, the day of rest and the time when we can pursue the things we love in life. This may be spending time with family and friends, playing sports, watching television or simply relaxing. Data also shows that we spend more time on social media at the weekend and specifically on a Sunday than at any other point during the week. If we are hoping to target a specific audience when they are more likely to notice our ads, the weekend is certainly the most effective time. Data analysis shows that sharing our content at this time will ensure it has the greatest social media reach. It must be noted, however, that as this knowledge becomes increasingly well known, other individuals, companies and businesses will also target their key messages at these times too. As a result, it's important to consider how you'll stand out from the other social media noise and chatter.

Individuals also use social media to share with others when they are in a good mood. Even if their social media posts don't always communicate that phrase exactly, by observing what activities they are involved in can be a fairly accurate representation. They may have just won a prize, booked a holiday, their team has just won a sports event, their partner has given birth, or they have just picked up a bargain from somewhere. These examples will all place them in a better mood making them more susceptible to your persuasive message or advertising. When observing these trends, it is also worth considering matching the correct type of message with the target audience mood too.

In 2015, professor of marketing Keith Wilcox from Columbia Business School recruited 142 participants to take part in an experiment involving mood congruence.[100] He split the participants into two groups, the first watching a clip from a movie about Einstein, which was deemed as neutral as it invoked no particular emotion in the viewer. The second group watched a more emotionally charged scene from the movie 'The Champ'. Both movies were then followed by an advert that either had an energetic tone to it or an advert with a moderately energetic tone to it.

When Wilcox and his team interviewed the participants afterwards to test their advert recall, they found that when the ad tone clashed with the tone of the movie that had preceded it, people paid less attention to the ad and therefore struggled to recall the information.

When the tone of the advert was matched with the tone of the movie clip they had watched before it, however, ad recall was 50% higher, and they watched it for much longer. This experiment clearly emphasises how the advert or persuasive message should be congruent with the context of the situation.

EXPERIMENT 62

The question:

When you go to a supermarket, do you find yourself buying the value items, the standard items or the luxury items? Other supermarkets may have different names for their segmented range, but which version do you gravitate towards and why?

VALUE / STANDARD / LUXURY

WHY?

The experiment:

One of my first jobs in sales was managing a fruit and vegetable department in one of the leading UK supermarkets. As part of my professional development, I visited a local procurement plant. Here they collected, washed and sorted apples (amongst other things). One thing that surprised me most at the time was that these apples finished being processed in one of two bags designated for one of two supermarkets. One of the bags of apples at the time was priced at £1.50 a bag and the other £3.50 a bag. These were the same apples, just in different bags. One was labelled as part of the value range of one supermarket, and the other was part of the luxury range of another. It wasn't until my love of the art of influence had taken hold, and I had conducted a few of my own experiments and researched many others did I begin to understand.

One of the most relevant experiments to help facilitate the explanation of this process was conducted by the psychologist Dan Ariely from Duke University in 2008.[101] In this experiment, he recruited 82 participants from Craigslist who were willing to take a painkiller and then receive two small electric shocks to test the effectiveness of the drug.

Ariely and his team explained that the first shock would be administered before taking the painkiller and the second shock after the painkiller. Half of the participants were told that the painkiller cost $2.50 per dose, whilst the other half were told it cost 10 cents a dose.

After the pills and had been taken and the shocks administered, Ariely and his team found that those participants who had taken the cheaper painkiller experienced 61% less pain than the first shock. In contrast, those who took the more expensive painkiller believed they experienced 85% less pain.

Whilst this demonstrates that the only variable was the price of the drug, what makes this an even more intriguing experiment and beautiful twist at the end was that both painkillers were, in fact, placebos. This demonstrates that it was simply the assumption that the more expensive painkiller would be more effective, and as a result, it gave the participants a distorted view of reality which translated into them feeling less pain.

In one of my masterclasses, I delivered in India, I mentioned the story above to some delegates, and one of them shared a similar story with me, which I think is a perfect addition here:

"People always come into my shop and ask for Ghee (clarified butter used extensively in Asian cooking). People would sometimes come in and not just ask for Ghee but my best Ghee, and I would have to explain to them that I only stocked one kind.

One day, a particularly assertive man came into my shop asking for my best Ghee which I duly gave and told him it was 15 rupees. The man then told him that he wanted the best and his friend had some Ghee at home that cost him 25 rupees. I told him that this is my best Ghee and it is all the same and is only 15 rupees. However, the customer did not want it. That evening I took my Ghee and divided it into four separate pots.

The next day the customer returned and asked if I had any better Ghee today. I said yes and presented him with the four tins. This one is 15 rupees, this one 17 rupees, this one 24 rupees and this one, my very best Ghee, for you, 25 rupees. (This was not a lie as I only had one quality of Ghee, and they were all the best). "This must certainly be the best", the customer said, having deceived himself by his own volition. He then asked me if he could offer me a discount on the promise that he will tell his friends. I agreed, and we negotiated a price of 21 rupees (for the same Ghee). He then told his friends to come and ask for me and mention his name, and I will give them a discount on my Ghee. He returns again and again, and my Ghee has never been so popular."

Whilst part of customers' demand for the best-priced Ghee was driven by his ego and his desire to feed it, this story also reiterates the fact that the assumption of the price of the Ghee was the thing that shaped his actual perception.

Principles of persuasion at work:

Rather than demonstrating any principles of persuasion, the examples above demonstrate that people can be easily influenced to buy something of a higher price based on their own assumption that it's of a higher quality. This allows us to understand why the more expensive painkillers were 'supposedly' more effective and why supermarkets can get away with putting the same apples in differently priced bags. There still has to be a baseline level of quality before you can consider giving them the same exposure as your higher-end products and services.

If you retain a high level of quality across your whole portfolio of products and services in a consistent manner, focussing your advertising and budget on your premium range can elevate the whole identity of your brand and be one which typifies luxury. This strategy has been used across all forms of marketing. Luxury car manufacturers have always struggled with how they can increase their market share with less expensive models without damaging the brands' exclusivity and luxury appeal. This was evident with Toyota's high-end brand, Lexus. Here, they tried to introduce a less expensive sedan that lacked the high-end features of its luxury range. However, this diluted Lexus' prestige brand image. Toyota was quick to react by upgrading their entry-level cars with sportier and more powerful features.

Whilst it can be beneficial to focus your brand on premium products and services, it's also important to offer people a range of options and to remember your market positioning so as not to undermine or dilute your brand image. Doing this allows you to have greater influence or persuasive power over a prospective client if they simply assume your product is of high quality, even if it isn't.

EXPERIMENT 63

The question:

Would you be more likely to commit to doing something if the request that was made was specific or more general in its nature?

SPECIFIC / GENERAL

The experiment:

In 2013, psychologist Katie Baca-Motes and her team of researchers from the University of California conducted an intriguing experiment at a hotel in Orange Country, California.[102] They wanted to explore what influences our commitment to certain causes and how it is possible to influence behaviour changes.

Over the course of the 31-week experiment, Baca-Motes and her team of researchers helped to check-in guests. Prior to issuing their room key, they gave some of them a form to fill out. The first group of guests were given a general question on their pre-check-in form, which asked them to 'check the box to indicate their willingness to be environmentally protective during their stay'. Of all of the guests asked, 98% agreed to this general commitment.

The second group were asked a more specific question. They were asked to 'check the box if they were willing to reuse their towels during their stay'. Of all the guests asked, 83% agreed to this more specific commitment.

(Based on the commitment rates at the front desk, it shows that if you want to influence or persuade people to either change or at the least, consider changing their actions and behaviours, it is better to give them a more general idea they can commit to than a specific one).

Alongside asking some of the guests to make a commitment, Baca-Motes and her team also distributed a number of 'Friends of the earth' pin badges at random to the new arrivals. With this, they wanted to see if wearing these badges would influence the guests' behaviour based on the box they had checked.

Finally, as with all well-constructed behavioural psychology experiments, there was also a control group who were neither asked to fill in a form nor given a pin badge.

Over the course of the following 31 weeks, the housekeeping staff fed back the actions and behaviours of the guests to the researchers.

They found that of the people who had checked the 'specific commitment box', 66% agreed to their commitment of being more environmentally conscious and reused their towels. This compared to 61% of the people who ticked the 'general commitment box' and reused their towels. Not only that but those guests, who had made a more specific commitment to reusing their towels, were also more environmentally friendly as well. Specifically, the housekeepers noted that they were more inclined not to use the air conditioning and switch the lights and TV off when they went out.

The pin badges also gave an additional dimension to the outcome of this experiment too.

Those who made a commitment and were given a badge were also more likely to reuse their towels than those making a commitment only. Furthermore, those same guests demonstrated more environmentally protective behaviours and acted as a reminder to others that they were part of a bigger 'movement' that wanted to preserve the environment.

Intriguingly, those guests wearing a pin badge (but making no commitment to being environmentally protective) were the least likely to reuse their towels, even more so than those not involved in the study at all.

Principles of persuasion at work:

It is consistency and commitment which are the principles of persuasion at work here. However, in order for a commitment to be delivered upon, it is essential that the person is both action-orientated and shares their commitment publicly.[103]

When influencing others, it is much more effective to encourage others to volunteer their commitment. When you have their voluntary buy-in, it's important to create a more specific action for them to pursue or target as well as providing them with the tools for them to publicly signal their commitment to others. By doing so, this will encourage others to voluntarily buy into the actions or behaviours you are trying to encourage and eventually create a snowball effect.

Whilst this approach works well in influencing external situations or people, internal situations or individuals may require a different approach. In the experiment detailed above, the researchers also noted that the housekeepers were inclined to change the towels regardless of their use or not. A similar approach could have been employed here too. One method would have been to actively encourage them to engage in a specific commitment and then, once they have bought into these commitments, demonstrate these same behaviours publicly to encourage buy-In from the other housekeepers too.

A two-step approach should be employed for any situation that requires your influence to gain a group commitment. The first would be to ensure the commitment is specific. The second approach is to include clues and cues that could be triggered and are related to the desired behaviours consistent with the initial specific commitment.[104] Examples may include:

If you want to influence a certain group of people to recycle more, put a recycling bin nearby.

If you want more people to help offset their carbon footprint, create a carpool scheme.

If you want your children to keep their bedroom tidy, put a bucket in their room to put their toys in.

EXPERIMENT 64

The question:

What are the funniest sitcoms you've seen?

What are the best movies you've seen?

The experiment:

The two questions above may seem out of place in a book examining the psychology and applications of influence, but there's an underlying reason. In 1983, German psychologist Norbert Schwarz and his colleagues wanted to explore a mental shortcut called 'availability heuristics'.[105]

An availability heuristic or mental shortcut takes our stored information and uses it to provide the best context for future predictions. Schwarz and his team gathered a group of participants to explore this and gave them two scenarios each.

The first group were asked to think of six instances when they behaved assertively and then, based on those instances, evaluate how assertive they are.

The second group were asked to think of twelve instances when they behaved assertively and then, based on those twelve, evaluate how assertive they are.

The evidence was clear those who had had to think of more instances described themselves as significantly less assertive than the participants who had to think of just six occasions where they behaved assertively. For both groups, it was only 3 or 4 occasions that came to mind easily. Those participants who were asked to think of twelve instances that they behaved assertively found it much more difficult to recall such a high number of occasions. This latter group associated that level of recall difficulty with their perceived level of assertiveness. Schwarz found that self-ratings were influenced by the ease with which the participants were able to recall the examples. The easier the instances were recalled, the greater influence it had on their own self-assessment of their assertiveness levels.

Principles of persuasion at work:

There are no direct principles of persuasion at work here, but the science shows that the availability heuristic can influence our judgements. We are persuaded by information that comes to mind most readily as opposed to the most accurate or informed answer.

Returning to the original question posed, if you think about the answers you gave, the funniest sitcoms or best movies you've seen are more likely to be the most recent ones, regardless of whether they are the funniest or best. If you look at online movie charts (such as IMDB), you will see how a large a percentage of the movies in the top fifty have been released in the last few years.

Similarly, if you were to ask peoples opinion on where the government should focus their money and resources, the reply is likely to be on issues that have or are affecting them personally or are at the forefront of their mind. This awareness is often highlighted by the media or others around them, thus keeping it relevant. In reality, whilst our personal issues or current news events, are important, they perhaps do not trump bigger issues affecting the world such as famine, human trafficking, global warming or nuclear development.

EXPERIMENT 65

The question:

Would you learn more effectively on a training programme that focussed on the past errors that other trainees had made or by the correct decisions and choices they'd made in the past?

MORE INFLUENCED BY PAST ERRORS / MORE INFLUENCED BY CORRECT DECISIONS MADE

The experiment:

In 2006, behavioural researcher Wendy Joung and her team wanted to gain an insight into the question above to examine the effectiveness of training programmes and which technique influences the trainees to learn more effectively.[106]

For this experiment, they recruited several firefighters to participate in the experiment due to the nature of their job requiring decisive decision-making abilities under intense stress. She split the firefighters into two groups, and each group was administered a different training programme. The first focussed on real-life situations. These examples detailed real-life events where the firemen had made poor decisions resulting in negative consequences. The second group, however, were presented with case studies that avoided these negative consequences and focussed more on the positive decisions made and positive outcomes as a result of these choices or decisions.

When Joung and her team made their evaluations at the end of the training programme, they found that the firefighters who had completed the error-based training had improved their judgement abilities and were able to think more adaptively than their counterparts who had followed the error-free case study training.

Principles of persuasion at work:

Whilst there are no immediate principles of persuasion at work here, the research supports a training style that focuses on the first-hand experience and uses error based examples. This style of training increases the trainee's attention and makes the training more memorable. This results in fewer errors and better decisions being made when this knowledge is implemented into the workplace.

The ability of a trainer and the strengths of the correct training package is a fundamental part of influencing teams to apply these learned behaviours to their work. Whilst many trainers and training packages focus on the positives of what the outcomes of a situation would be if you take the correct action, the above evidence shows that delivering a training programme which focusses on the negatives that incorrect action would have, is even more influential and successful in delivering the training's main message.

These messages can be communicated through videos, personal accounts and case studies of the situations in question. This can be the perfect fuel to stimulate a conversation within the trainee groups for them to decide upon the most appropriate action they would take. As mentioned, the most effective way of doing this is by highlighting the negative consequences caused by these poor decisions. Using this technique, hypothetical situations such as these (or even first-hand experiences or testimonials) can also be applied in the classroom, to sports coaches and to children to increase their abilities and effectiveness.

Football managers can look at why their team or other teams concede goals the way that they did and the consequences they had on the rest of the game. Parents can highlight the dangers of their children speaking to strangers and the consequences based on that. Finally, teachers can highlight to their students the need to pass exams and study hard by using students who failed to do so and the current lives they are leading now as an example to the rest of the class.

BONUS EXPERIMENT

The question:

Based on other examples and evaluations in this book, how would you lead a minority group to persuade the majority group that your principles and beliefs are correct? How would you achieve this to the point where your influence holds such strength, your group becomes the majority?

HOW WOULD YOU DO IT?

The experiment:

I thought to finish this book, it would be apt to look at how a minority group can influence a majority group. Perhaps the most well-known example of a minority group overcoming the majority is the movement for women to have voting rights in 1903. This was otherwise known as the Suffragette movement and is the perfect example of 'minority influence'. Minority influence occurs when a small group (or minority) influences a larger group (or majority).

In 1969, psychologists Serge Moscovici and Marisa Zavalloni conducted an experiment to see if a consistent minority could influence a majority to give an incorrect answer in a colour perception task.[107]

For this experiment, 172 female participants were told that they were taking part in a colour perception test. The participants took part in the experiments in groups of 4, with an additional two participants. These additional 2 participants were actually 2 of Moscovici's researchers playing the role of participants. These two researchers (stooges) were essential to this experiment as they were playing the role of the minority group whilst the genuine participants were acting as the majority group. A second group was formed to act as the control group and was made up of no confederates and only the genuine participants.

In the first round of the experiment, all six participants were shown 36 blue coloured slides of all different intensities and asked to name the colour they saw. The two confederates answered 'green' for all the slides whilst the other participants made their own independent guesses.

In the second round, the confederate participants answered that they thought 24 of the slides were 'green' whilst the other 12 slides were 'blue'. As you can see, the confederates offered a more inconsistent set of answers in this round. Again, the genuine participants made their own independent guesses.

In the first experiment, despite being the minority group, the confederates had managed to influence 8% of the participants into agreeing that the slides were green. In the second experiment, where their answers were more inconsistent, only 1% of the genuine participants answered that the slides were green.

Principles of persuasion at work:

Commitment and consistency are the two principles of persuasion at work here. In behavioural psychology, it is agreed that there are two forms of consistency that are applicable to a minority group successfully influencing a majority group. Whilst the experiment above shows the minority group influencing 8% of the majority, this percentage could be much higher depending on the openness to be influenced by the majority group or a minority group that had great numbers compared to the majority group.

The first is Diachronic consistency. This is pressure applied on the majority group by the minority group over a period of time when the majority are inflexible with their stance. The second form of consistency is synchronic consistency, in which all members of the minority group agree and back each other up.

Moscovici believed that consistency is the most important element for a minority group to overcome the majority and can do this by adhering to their principles and beliefs without wavering.[108] By doing so, this creates certainty and stability within the group and results in the majority, regardless of their intention to change, being forced to take notice and question their own stance. By questioning their own position, it creates an element of uncertainty and doubt within themselves and their own group. In turn, this potentially destabilises or disrupts their social norms.

It is the strength, self-confidence and self-belief to stand up against the norm which plants an element of self-doubt in the majority. By encouraging the majority group to doubt itself, it specifically encourages them to question their own commitment and allegiance to the majority.

If the majority are flexible, compromising and open-minded, then the minority have an increased chance of exerting their influence with success. If one member of the majority begins to agree with the minority, then this can influence others within the group resulting in a snowball effect that ends up being compounded by another principle of persuasion – consensus.

Moscovici is quite correct when he earmarks consistency as the most important principle of persuasion for a minority group to hold.[109] If they are clear on their requests and needs and have a unified voice to support these requirements, then this will create certainty within their own group but uncertainty in the opposing group. Once a few members of the majority decide to switch allegiances, and the snowball effect takes hold, the minority will soon become the majority, and over time, people will not even remember where the original view, stance or opinion originated from.[110]

This understanding can be applied in your personal, social or professional life. Suppose your family really wanted to order a takeaway for the weekend, but you wanted a change of scenery, a more refined meal, and something where all the family can be together without the distractions of the TV, social media and the like. With you being in the minority, it is important that you communicate the same message again and again and be committed to your stance. This will demonstrate to your family (the majority) your commitment to the idea of eating out. If you were to support that with a plan of some restaurants you could go to, the menu choices and maybe something to do after dinner such as bowling or the movies, then you may be able to leverage your influence through their flexibility. Much like in the example, the key here is to deliver a consistent and unwavering message and stance.

CONCLUSION

Congratulations on getting to the end! Genuinely!

Statistically, less than 10% of people make it past the first chapter of most non-fiction books. They buy it, read a few pages, paragraphs or a couple of chapters, begin to feel they have learnt enough, and then put it to one side. You, on the other hand, have read to the end, so congratulations!

I genuinely hope you found some value in what I have shared.

I hope you found that the experiments I hand-picked for this book were enjoyable, intriguing and inspiring. I also hope that you feel confident to use the ideas, tips and learnings from each experiment in your own personal, social or professional life. You can do so knowing that they are guaranteed to work because they are supported by the science behind influence and persuasion. In the business arena, where I deliver most of my keynotes, sessions and masterclasses, all of the influence skills you find in this book can be easily applied and employed in all areas of business, including leadership, motivation, decision making, management, coaching, communication and problem-solving.

I'm sure you'll agree that this book delves into so much more than just the concept of influence. It's my sincere wish that you dip in and out of this book and treat it as a manual or handbook if you are looking for a technique for inspiring change, increasing your profits, communicating a message, or bringing more customers to your bricks and mortar or online store. These same tips can be employed in your personal life as well to influence your friends to go to the restaurant of your choice or encourage your children to tidy away their toys as well as many other situations.

I hope that this book will also encourage you to look at life a little bit differently and help you understand why people behave the way that they do. This may make you more tolerant, more understanding and ultimately, more effective.

I guarantee that if you employ these influence techniques and principles correctly, they will increase your effectiveness in your private and professional life. This will result in more effective teams and family relationships. The experiments and insights I have shared in this book can help:

Salespeople influence their prospective customers

Managers influence their staff

Coaches to influence their players

Parents to influence their children

Politicians to influence their electorate

Marketing consultants to influence consumers

Health professionals to influence patients

Leaders to influence their followers

Activists to influence the masses

and more.....

Even if you are in one of the positions above and have spent your entire career persuading and influencing people, it is my sincere hope that you can find even more influence applications or techniques inside these pages that either you didn't know or can build on your existing skill-set.

I am fortunate to have been able to share my knowledge and expertise with companies all over the world through keynotes, workshops, and masterclasses, and my audience ranges from Directors and CEOs to salesmen and new teams. I don't profess to know everything about the psychology of influence, so much so that one of my highlights of attending these events alongside sharing my knowledge is speaking with the delegates to understand their insights and applications of the principles of persuasion. One of my favourite stories that I share with delegates, workshop attendees, or clients is about a boilermaker.

Once upon a time, there was a 'Boilermaker' (engineer) who was hired to fix a boiler on a steamship that was not working well. The boilermaker listened to the list of problems, asked a few questions then went below. After fifteen minutes of examining the maze of pipes and steam escaping, he took out a small hammer and gave a little tap on a little red valve, and the boiler started working perfectly. On completion of his work, he presented the steamship owner with a bill for one thousand dollars. The owner was enraged by this hefty price tag for just fifteen minutes of work, complained to the engineer, and demanded an itemised bill. He redrafted the bill stating that the tap with his hammer was charged at 50 cents, and the knowledge and years' experience of knowing where to tap was billed at $999.50, bringing the total to $1000.

Much the same as this book and the tips and techniques I have shared with you - if you are open to new influence principles and applications, then it's just a little tap using the correct techniques in the correct places without having to pick up a full toolbox, that will supercharge your effectiveness not only in your professional life but your social and personal life too.

A LITTLE THANK YOU

Influence and persuasion are incredible passions of mine, and knowing that my knowledge may potentially help even more people and have a far greater reach than my current work, is humbling, so thank you. Thank you also for having the courage to buy this book when that same money could have bought a mug or a chocolate bar.

I would love to hear if you found the contents useful, and it would really help if you could spread the word or share this book with your friends, write a review or encourage your friends or colleagues to buy a copy. If you or they are interested in my masterclasses, workshops, keynote presentations or influence demonstration shows, then it would be great to connect.

Similarly, if you have any thoughts or suggestions, I'd love to chat with you at the end of one of my keynotes or on one of my masterclasses. I'm really approachable and have a thirst for learning and sharing all elements of this beautiful art of influence.

Even if you just want some free updates to accompany this book as I discover new principles, experiments and applications, drop me an email, and I'll be happy to oblige.

I look forward to hearing from you,

Duncan Stevens

www.duncanstevens.com

ABOUT THE AUTHOR

Duncan has been working in the field of influence for over a decade. As a master of influence and founder of the Influence Association, he is in high demand across Europe, America and the UK as a keynote speaker and trainer. He travels the world delivering keynotes, workshops and masterclasses.

In doing so, Duncan helps companies develop strategies and tools using his knowledge of people, the mental shortcuts they take and their patterns of behaviour to make them more effective and increase overall commercial success.

His sessions cover influence, body language, leadership, sales, management, motivation, innovation, decision making, communication, problem-solving, and online presence and persuasion.

The bulk of his consulting and speaking work looks at applying and employing these concepts to help others perform more efficiently and achieve a shift in consumer and employee thinking and perception. All of his work is underpinned by decades of research and evidence that has been tried and tested and peer-reviewed. In this way, clients can be assured they are getting solutions and techniques which are more than just anecdotal and hearsay - they actually work.

Duncan works with small and large companies as well as delivering interactive after-dinner shows which are 100% entertainment and have a focus on influence, persuasion and human psychology.

Similar to his show, all of Duncan's keynotes, training sessions and masterclasses are interactive and engaging so that his clients, delegates or attendees are guaranteed to leave any of the sessions with something actionable right then and there to make them more effective and influential.

If you want to reach out and say hi, share your thoughts on the book or for anything else, you can find Duncan on one of your preferred social media platforms:

Connect with Duncan on LinkedIn:

https://www.linkedin.com/in/duncanstevensinfluence/

For pictures and video clips, find him on Instagram:

https://www.instagram.com/duncanstevensofficial/

For booking enquiries, blog posts and more, find him online:

https://www.duncanstevens.com/

A LITTLE ASK

The purpose of this book is to help others become more persuasive, influential and effective in their work and personal lives. If the principles, techniques and tools shared in this book are applied, then this will lead to a much richer, fulfilled and abundant life.

At the time of writing (2020), the world is struggling to cope with the demands placed upon it. I hope that this little book can bring some confidence, joy and effectiveness to all of those who read it.

I was wondering if you could do me a little favour. Most people search for this book on Amazon, and I was wondering if you could write a couple of sentences in the form of a review on the Amazon page for me. It's really quick and easy and would help lots in getting my book into the hands of the people it could really benefit.

On the subject of helping one another out, I thought this would be a good place as any to let you know how I can help you out if you wanted to order bulk copies of this book. At the start of this project, I opted to hold on to the publishing rights. This allows me to make changes and updates to the book as the latest experiments are conducted in the field of influence and persuasion. Not only that, but it also means that if you wanted to order bulk copies of this book, I could provide you with big savings compared to its' normal retail cost.

If this is something that is of interest to you, you can email me directly at **duncan@duncanstevens.com** for more information.

NOTES

[1] Costa, P. T., and McCrae, R. R. (1985). The NEO Personality Inventory manual. Odessa, FL: Psychological Assessment Resources.

[2] Morris, M. W., Podolny, J., and Ni Sullivan, B. (2008). Culture and co-worker relations: Interpersonal patterns in American, Chinese, German, and Spanish divisions of a global retail bank. Organization Science, 19(4), 517–532.

[3] Moriarty, T. (1975). Crime, commitment, and the responsive bystander: Two field experiments. Journal of Personality and Social Psychology, 31(2), 370–376.

[4] Lankford, A., Madfis, E. (2018). "Media Coverage of Mass Killers: Content, Consequences, and Solutions". American Behavioral Scientist. 62 (2): 151–162.

[5] Ross, L., Greene, D., and House, P. (1977). The false consensus phenomenon: An attributional bias in self-perception and social perception processes. Journal of Experimental Social Psychology, 13, 279-301.

[6] Trope, Y., and Bassok, M. (1983). Information-gathering strategies in hypothesis testing, Journal of Experimental Social Psychology, 19 (6) 560-576.

[7] Dutton, K. (2011). Flipnosis: The Art of Split-Second Persuasion, Cornerstone Digital.

[8] Dutton, K. (2010). Flipnosis: The Art of Split-Second Persuasion (Stevens Heinemann).

[9] Beyth-Marom, R., and Dekel, S. (1985). An elementary approach to thinking under certainty. Hillsdale, NJ: Erlbaum.

[10] McCleneghan, J Sean. (2003). Selling sex to college females: Their attitudes about Cosmopolitan and Glamour magazines, The social science Journals, 40 pp 317-325.

[11] Dion, K., Berscheid, E., and Walster, E. (1972). "What is beautiful is good" Journal of personality and social psychology 24, no.3, 285-90.

[12] Ash, S. E. (1952). "Group Forces in the Modification and Distortion of Judgements" Social Psychology 450-501.

[13] Rind, B., and Strohmetz, D. (2001). "Effect on Restaurant Tipping of Presenting Customers with an interesting task and of reciprocity" Journal of applied social psychology 31, no.7, 1379-384.

[14] Festinger, L., and Carlsmith, J.M., (1959). "Cognitive Consequences of Forced Compliance". The Journal of Abnormal and Social Psychology 58, no. 2: 203-10.

[15] Oppenheimer, D.M. (2005). 'Consequences of Erudite Vernacular Utilized Irrespective of Necessity: Problems With Using Long Words Needlessly'. Journal of applied cognitive Psychology, 20, 139-56.

[16] Cialdini, R. B. (1993). Influence: Science and Practice. New York: Harper Collins College Publishers.

[17] Kang, Min Jeong, Ming Hsu, Ian M.Krajbich, George Loewenstein, Samuel M. McClure, Joseph Tao-yi Wang and Colin F. Canerer. "The Wick in the Candle of Learning: Epistemic Curiosity Activates Reward Circuitry and Enhances Memory". Psychological Science 20, no. 8 (2009) 963-73.

[18] Skinner, B.F. (1948). "Superstition' in the Pigeon". Journal of Experimental Psychology 38, no.2: 168-72.

[19] Sherif, M. (1954). Experimental Study of Positive and Negative Intergroup Attitudes Between Experimentally Produced Groups: Robbers Cave Study. Norman, OK.

[20] Tversky, A. and Kahneman, D. (1986). Rational Choice and the Framing of Decisions. Ft. Belvoir: Defense Technical Information Center.

[21] Cialdini, R. B., et al. (1975). "Reciprocal Concessions Procedure for Inducing Compliance: The Door-in-the-Face-Technique". Journal of Personality and Social Psychology 31, no. 2: 206-15.

[22] Jostmann, Nils B., Daniel Lakens, and Thomas W. Schubert. "Weight as an Embodiment of Importance". "Psychological Science 20, no. 9 (2009): 1169-174.

[23] Quin, K. O., Aronoff. J. (1981). Humour as a technique of social influence'. Social psychology Quarterly, 44, 349-57.

[24] Carnevale, P., Isen, A. M. (1986). "The influence of positive affect and visual access on the discovery of integrative solutions in bilateral negotiation." Organizational Behavior and Human Decision Processes 37(1), 1-13.

[25] Lepper, M. R., Greene, D., and Nisbett, R. E. (1973) Undermining children's intrinsic interest with extrinsic reward: A test of the "over-justification" hypothesis. Journal of Personality and Social Psychology, 28(1), 129–137

[26] Higgins, C.A and Judge, T.A (2004). "The Effect of Applicant Influence Tactics on Recruiter Perceptions of Fit and Hiring Recommendations: A Field Study" Journal of Applied Psychology, 89, 622-32.

[27] Oppenheimer, D.M and Atler, A. (2006). 'Predicting short-term stock fluctuations by using processing fluency'. Proceedings of the National Academy of Sciences, USA, 103, 9369-72.

[28] Raghubi, P. and Valenzuela, A. (2006). 'Centre-of-Inattention: Position Biases in Decision-Making'. Organisational Behaviour and Human Decision Processes, 99, 66-80.

[29] Jones, E. and Gordon, E. (1972). 'Timing of self-disclosure and its' effects on personal attraction'. Journal of personality and social psychology, 24, 358-609.

[30] Sanders, T. (2005). The Likeability Factor, New York: Crown Publishers.

[31] Jecker, J. and Landy, D. (1969). Liking a person as a function of doing him a favor. Human relations, 22, 371-78.

[32] Aronson, E., Willerman, B., and Floyd., J (1966). The effect of pratfall on increasing interpersonal attractiveness. Psychonomic Science, 4, 227-8.

[33] Kahneman, D., Knetsch, J., and Thaler, R. (1991). "Anomalies: The endowment effect, loss aversion, and status quo bias," Journal of Economic Perspectives, 5(1), 193-206.

[34] Carmon, Z., and Ariely, D., (2000). "Focusing on the Forgone: How Value Can Appear So Different to Buyers and Sellers," Journal of Consumer Research, 27 (December), 360-70.

[35] Kahneman, D., Knetsch, J., and Thaler, R. (2008). "The Endowment Effect: Evidence of Losses Valued More than Gains," Handbook of Experimental Economics Results, 1 (7), 939-948.

[36] Fointiat, V. (2000). "Foot-in-the-Mouth" Versus "Door-in-the-Face" Requests, the Journal of Social Psychology, 140:2.

[37] McGlone, M.S., and Tofighbakhsh, J. (2000). Birds of a Feather Flock Conjointly: Rhyme as Reason in Aphorisms. Psychological science, 11, 424-8.

[38] Chandler, J., and Schwarz, N. (2008). How extending your middle finger affects your perception of others: Learned Journal of Experimental Social Psychology.

[39] Wells, G.L, Petty, R.E (1980). The effects of overt head movements on persuasion: Compatibility and incompatibility of responses. Basic and applied social psychology, 1, 219-230.

[40] Tom, G. Peterson, P., Lau, Y., Burton, T., and Cook, J. (1991). The role of overt head movement in the formation of affect. Basic and applied social psychology, 12, 281-9.

[41] Sagarin, B. J., Cialdini, R.B., Rice, W.E., and Sherman B. S. (2002). "Dispelling the Illusion of invulnerability: The motivations and mechanisms of resistance to persuasion". Journal of personality and social psychology 83, no .3: 526-41.

[42] Latane, B. and Darley, J.M (1968). Group inhibition of Bystander Intervention in Emergencies. Journal of Personality and Social Psychology, 10, 215-21.

[43] Regan, D.T (1971). Effects of a favour and liking on compliance. Journal of experimental social psychology, 7, 627-39.

[44] Kunz, P.R., Woolcott, M. (1976). Seasons Greetings: From my status to yours. Social science research, 5, 269-78.

[45] Hornstein, H.A., Fisch, E., and Holmes, M. (1968). Influence of a Model's feeling about his behaviour and his relevance as a comparison on other observers' helping behaviour. Journal of Personality and social psychology, 10, 3, 222-6.

[46] Freedman. J.L., and Fraser, S.C. (1966). Compliance without pressure: The foot in the door technique. Journal of personality and social psychology, 4, 196-202.

[47] Batson, C.D., Thompson, E.R., and Chen, H. (2002). Moral hypocrisy: Addressing some alternatives. Journal of personality and social psychology, 83, 330-9.

[48] Batson, C.D., Thompson, E.R., Seuferling, G., Whitney, H., and Strongman, J. (1999). 'Moral hypocrisy: Appearing moral to oneself without being so.' Journal of personality and social psychology, 77, 525-37.

[49] R. Garner (2005). 'Post-It-Note Persuasion: A sticky influence' Journal of Consumer Psychology, 15, pages 230-7.

[50] Williams, L.E., and Bargh, J.A. (2008). Experiencing physical warmth promotes interpersonal warmth. Science, 322, 606-7.

[51] Zhong, C.B and Leonardelli, G.J. (2008). Experiencing physical warmth promotes interpersonal warmth. Science, 322, 606-7.

[52] Strohmetz, D. B., Rind, B., Fisher, R., and Lynn, M. (2002). Sweetening the till the use of candy to increase restaurant tipping. Journal of Applied Social Psychology, 32: 300–309.

[53] Burger, J. M. (1986). Increasing compliance by improving the deal: The that's-not-all technique. Journal of Personality and Social Psychology.

[54] Elms, A.C. (1966). Influence of fantasy ability change through role-playing. Journal of personality and social psychology, 4, 36-43.

[55] Zimbardo, P. (1972). Pathology of imprisonment. Society, 9, 4-8.

[56] Janis, I.L and King, B.T. (1954). The influence of role-playing on opinion change. Journal of abnormal social psychology, 49, 211-18.

[57] Hatfield, E., Cacioppo, J.T and Rapson, R.L (1994). Emotional Contagion. New York: Cambridge University Press.

[58] Friedman, H.S and Riggio, R. (1981). The effect of individual differences in nonverbal expressiveness on transmission of emotion. Journal of nonverbal behaviour, 6, 96-104.

[59] Andreasson, P., and Dimberg, U. (2008). Emotional empathy and facial feedback. Journal of nonverbal behaviour, 32, 215-24 and Dimberg, U., Andreasson, P., and Thunberg, M. (2011) Emotional empathy and facial reactions to facial expressions. Journal of psychophysiology. 25, 26-31.

[60] Aronson, E., Blaney, N., Sikes, J., Stephan, C., and Snapp, M. (1975). Busing and racial tension: The jigsaw route to learning and liking, Psychology Today, 8, 43-59.

[61] Rosenthal R., and Jacobson, L. (1968). Pygmalion in the classroom: Teacher expectations and pupils' intellectual development. Holt Reinhart and Winston, New York.

[62] Wells, G.L (1988). Eyewitness identification: A system handbook. Carswell, Toronto.

[63] Orne, M. T., and Evans, F. J. (1965). Social control in the psychological experiment: Antisocial behaviour and hypnosis. Journal of Personality and Social Psychology, 1(3), 189–200.

[64] Gibson, H.B. (1991) Can hypnosis compel people to commit harmful, immoral and criminal acts? A review of literature'. Contemporary Hypnosis, 8, 129-40.

[65] Festinger, L., Riecken, H.W., and Schachter, S. (1956). When prophecy fails: A social and psychological study of a modern group that predicted the destruction of the world. University of Minnesota Press, Minneapolis, MN.

[66] Cialdini, R.B., Demaine, L.J., Sagarin, B.J., Barrett, D.W., Rhoads, K., and Winter, P. (2006). Managing social norms for persuasive impact. Social Influence, 1(1), 3-15.

[67] Goldstein, N. J., Cialdini, R. B., and Griskevicius, V. (2008). A Room with a viewpoint: Using social norms to motivate environmental conservation in hotels. Journal of Consumer Research, 35(3), 472-482.

[68] Raghubir, P. (2004). Free gift with purchase: Promoting or discounting the brand? Journal of Consumer Psychology, 14, 181–86.

[69] Leventhal, H., Singer, R., and Jones, S. (1965). Effects of fear and specificity of recommendation upon attitudes and behaviour. Journal of Personality and Social Psychology, (2), 20–29.

[70] Garner, R. (2005). Post-It® Note persuasion: a sticky influence. Journal of Consumer Psychology, 15,230–37.

[71]Brehm, J.W. (1960). Attitudinal consequences of commitment to unpleasant behaviour. Journal of abnormal and social psychology, 60, 370-83.

[72] Freedman, J. L., and Fraser, S. C. (1966). Compliance without pressure: The foot-in-the-door technique. Journal of Personality and Social Psychology, 4:195–203.

[73] Bickman, L. (1972). Environmental attitudes and actions, Journal of Social Psychology, 87, 323-4.

[74] Knox, R. E., and Inkster, J. A. (1968). Post-decision dissonance at post time. Journal of Personality and Social Psychology, 8(4, Pt.1), 319–323

[75] Brehm, J. W., and Cohen, A. R. (1962). Explorations in cognitive dissonance. John Wiley and Sons Inc.

[76] Maddux, W. W., Mullen, E., and Galinsky, A. D. (2008). Chameleons bake bigger pies and take bigger pieces: Strategic behavioral mimicry facilitates negotiation outcomes. Journal of Experimental Social Psychology, 44:461–68.

[77] Chartrand, T.K., and Bargh, J. A. (1999). The Chameleon Effect: the perception-behaviour link and social interaction. Journal of Personality and Social Psychology, 76:893–910.

[78] van Baaren, R.B., Holland, R.W., Kawakami, K., and van Knippenberg, A. (2004). Mimicry and Prosocial Behavior, Psychological Science, Vol. 15, No. 1: pp. 71-74.

[79] Langer, E., Blank, A., and Chanowitz, B. (1978). The mindlessness of ostensibly thoughtful action: The role of “placebic” information in interpersonal interaction. Journal of Personality and Social Psychology, 36:639–42.

[80] Langer, E., Blank, A., and Chanowitz, B. (1978). The mindlessness of ostensibly thoughtful action: The role of “placebic” information in interpersonal interaction. Journal of Personality and Social Psychology, 36:639–42.

[81] Tormala, Z. L., and Petty, R. E. (2007). Contextual contrast and perceived knowledge: Exploring the implications for persuasion. Journal of Experimental Social Psychology, 43:17–30.

[82] Beaman, A. L., Klentz, B., Diener, E., and Svanum, S. (1979). Self-awareness and transgression in children: Two field studies. Journal of Personality and Social Psychology, 37:1835–46.

[83] Kallgren, C. A., Reno, R. R., and Cialdini, R. B. (2000). A focus theory of normative conduct: When norms do and do not affect behavior. Personality and Social Psychology Bulletin, 26:1002–12.

[84] Petrova, P. K., Cialdini, R. B., and Sills, S. J. (2007). Consistency-based compliance across cultures. Journal of Experimental Social Psychology, 43:104–11.

[85] Cialdini, R. B., Wosinska, W., Barrett, D. W., Butner, J., and Gornik-Durose, M. (1999). Compliance with a request in two cultures: The differential influence of social proof and commitment/consistency on collectivists and individualists. Personality and Social Psychology Bulletin, 25:1242–53.

[86] Miyamoto, Y., and Schwarz, N. (2006). When conveying a message may hurt the relationship: Cultural differences in the difficulty of using an answering machine. Journal of Experimental Social Psychology, 42:540–47.

[87] Scollon, R., and Scollon, S. W. (1995). Intercultural Communication: A Discourse Approach. Cambridge, UK: Blackwell.

[88] White, S. (1989). Backchannels across cultures: A study of Americans and Japanese. Language in Society, 18: 59–76.

[89] Goldstein, N.J., Cialdini, R.B., and Griskevicius, V. (2008). A Room with a Viewpoint: Using Social Norms to Motivate Environmental Conservation in Hotels. Journal of Consumer Research Vol 35: 3, pages 472-482.

[90] Milgram, S. (1974). Obedience to authority: An experimental view. New York: Harper and Row.

[91] McCabe, D. P., and Castel, A.D (2008). "Seeing is believing: The Effect of Brain Images on Judgements of Scientific Reasoning". Cognition 107, no. 1: 343-52.

[92] D.J. Howard (1990). The influence of verbal responses to common greetings on compliance behaviour: The Foot in The Mouth effect'. Journal of applied social psychology, 20, 1185-96.

[93] Rothman, A.J, and Kiviniemi, M. (1999). Treating people with health information: an analysis and review of approaches to communicating health risk information. Journal of the National Cancer Institute Monographs 25: 44-51.

[94] Darley, J., and Batson, D. (1973). 'From Jerusalem to Jericho', Journal of Personality and Social Psychology, Vol. 27, No. 1, pp. 100–108.

[95] Ross, L., and Nisbett, R.E. (1991). The Person and the Situation: Perspectives of Social Psychology. Front Cover. Temple University Press.

[96] Hoffman, B. (2015). Marketers Are From Mars, Consumers Are From New Jersey.

[97] Wood, W., Quinn, J. and Kashy, D. (2002). 'Habits in Everyday Life: Thought, Emotion, and Action' [Journal of Personality and Social Psychology, Vol. 83, No. 6, pp. 1281–1297.

[98] Shotton, R. (2018). The Choice Factory: 25 behavioural biases that influence what we buy. Harriman House Publishing.

[99] Roach, T., Mawdsley, C., and Dorsett, J. (2008). 'Sainsbury's – How an idea helped make Sainsbury's great again'.

[100] Bronner, F., Bronner, J., Faasse, J. (2007). 'In the Mood for Advertising', International Journal of Advertising, Vol. 26, No. 3, 2007.

[101] Puccinelli, N., Wilcox., and Grewal, D. (2015). 'Consumers' Response to Commercials: When the Energy Level in the Commercial Conflicts with the Media Context', Journal of Marketing, Vol. 79, No. 2, pp. 1–18.

[102] Waber, R., Shiv, B., Carmon, Z., and Ariely, D (2008). 'Commercial Features of Placebo and Therapeutic Efficacy', Journal of the American Medical Association, Vol. 299, No.9, pp. 1016–1017.

[103] Baca-Motes, K., Brown, A., Gneezy, A., Keenan, E.A., and Nelson, L.D. (2013). Commitment and Behavior Change: Evidence for the Field. Journal of Consumer Research DOI: 10.1086/667226.

[104] Cialdini, R.B., Influence – Science and Practice 5th Edition (2009). Allyn and Bacon. New York.

[105] Goldstein, N.J., Cialdini, R.B., and Griskevicius, V. (2008). A Room with a Viewpoint: Using Social Norms to Motivate Environmental Conservation in Hotels. Journal of Consumer Research Vol 35: 3, pages 472-482.

[106] Schwarz, N., Bless, H., Strack, F., Klumpp, G., Rittenauer-Schakta, H., and Simons, A. (1983). Ease of retrieval as information and directive functions of affective states. Journal of Personality and Social Psychology, 45, pp 513-523.

[107] Joung, W., Hesketh, B., and Neal, A. (2006). Using "war stories" to train for adaptive performance: Is it better to learn from error or success? Applied Psychology: An International Review, 55, 282–302.

[108] Moscovici, S. and Zavalloni, M. (1969). The group as a polarizer of attitudes. Journal of Personality and Social Psychology, 12, 125-135.

[109] Moscovici, S. (1976). Social influence and social change. London: Academic Press.

[110] Moscovici, S. (1980). Toward a theory of conversion behavior. In L. Berkowitz (Ed.), Advances in experimental social psychology (Vol. 13, (pp. 209–239). New York: Academic Press.

Made in the USA
Monee, IL
18 March 2024

55270986R00168